De

I would like to thank ~~my~~ ~~~~ ~~~~ their encouragement. Without them, I couldn't have written this book.

There are two special people who have kept me driving on. The first is my loving and beautiful wife Cynthia. Since that December night of our wedding, she has encouraged me in all things in life. She has proof read all of my stories, made corrections and suggestions. She even told me a few of the stories that I've added in the book.

The second person that has encouraged me is my daughter Tami who was a drama and English teacher. She found writers' conferences that she and I attended and gave pointers on writing styles and technique. She kept telling me, "You can do it Dad. Just keep writing."

Thanks again to everyone for their encouragement.

Introduction

My name is Michael Humphries; I was born and raised near DeKalb, Texas in a small community called Hubbard Chapel. One of the best things the Lord gave me was good memory. I have always loved old stories, some funny, some true to life. I remember my grandparents and the things they did for a living. I loved their old home place which was a second home to me. My parents had some stories for me; my dad contributed a lot. He had a very hard life growing up. Many other relatives contributed also.

I work at Red River Army Depot starting in 1976 and took an early retirement in 1997, drove a truck for 3 ½ years after that and got a call one day from my old boss asking if I wanted to come back to work for him as a contractor at Red River. I said, "Sure," truck driving was literally about to kill me, sixteen to eighteen hour days are tough. Some of stories come from my Red River experience and some from truck driving.

How I got started writing short stories, my daughter who was a drama and English teacher bought me two books for Christmas of 2000. One was Puncher Pie and Cowboy Lies written by Steven Sederwall and Chicken Wing Fling by Mitchel Whittington. I read them by candle light during the ice storm of 2000 and 2001. These are some of the funniest books I have ever read and heartily encourage you read them, right after you read mine. After telling my daughter how much I enjoyed the books, she said, "Dad you ought to write down some of your stories." That was twelve years ago and I'm still writing. My daughter and I have been to several writing seminars and conferences. She is really the one with the true writer's talent but has written very little. I remember a small article she wrote about my mother-in-law and how she painted the scene with words. She has inspired me to do the same.

I recall all of my stories as if they were yesterday, those that are mine that is. I love to gather and collect stories. You may ask how a person gets these stories. Someone will say, "You ought to go and talk to so and so, they will have a ton of stories to tell." But when you go and ask them they will tell you, "I don't know any stories." If you want to hear stories find a bunch of old men sitting around a coffee pot or perhaps women setting around sewing on a quilt. Another place for stories to boil over or spring to life is for old men in their bib overalls sitting around a warm wood burning potbellied stove using an old coffee can for spittoon. A lot of these old men would be retired farmers, long time loggers or perhaps truck drivers. When it comes down to it, everyone has a story, probably many in fact. I like to be like a fly on the wall, so to speak, not saying a word but sit back and just listen and gather all of it in.

After I starting writing I was looking for a publisher. All of them wanted money up front with me doing most of the work. I probably looked close to ten years for a publisher, one fall day I saw Shari Parker's advertised as a publisher so I contacted her. She has been what I have been looking for in a publisher. I know nothing about publisher a book, but Shari does and she does all of the work. I just provide the stories. But I'm still nervous, I often worried that my stories are not interesting enough. I remember reading Elmer Kelton's The Time It Never Rained. It started off slow and dull but before it was over I wanted to craw in that book and start helping those people, get involved in their lives. I want my book to be so good that it makes people to want craw into my book and experience what I have. Shari assures me my stories are interesting. She does a good job of propping me up. She created the title and designed the cover. I let a friend see it and she said she said would buy the book just from seeing the cover. It makes you want to see what is inside.

My goal is to live life to the fullest. What does that mean? To me that means being the Christian God called me to be. I love to laugh and make people laugh. I think Jesus wants us to have a good sense of humor.

I guess I have evolved into a storyteller of some sorts. My hero of storytellers is the late Jerry Clowers and my favor tale of his was how Marcel went to visit Uncle Vercee and Aunt Nel on a Sunday afternoon. Marcel stayed until it was close to supper time. Aunt Nel asked, "Won't you stay and have supper with us, we're have fried chicken?" Now Aunt Nel's fried chicken would put Colonel Sanders to shame. It was Blue Ribbon county fair winning fried chicken, finger lickin good. Well, Uncle Vercee and Aunt Nel had six kids and with that many there wasn't a lot to go around the second time. Just so happen no one noticed but a storm had been brewing up, real quick like. Now this was before rural folk had electricity and all they had for light was a hanging coal oil lamp. Just so happen there was one piece of fried chicken left and everyone was eyeing it. All of a sudden that storm came up with a strong wind and blew out the coal oil lamp since the windows were all open. You never in all your life heard a blood curdling scream after the lamp was out. They finally got the lamp lit again. They found what the blood curdling scream was all about and that was Marcel had eight forks in his hand.

I hope you enjoy the stories in my book. I am writing the second book now. Get a comfy chair, a big glass of sweet tea and this book. You will be there for the entire afternoon.

God Bless,

Michael Humphries

Tales From

My Rocker

Michael Humphries

Shari Parker
Publishing & Printing

This is a work of fiction. The characters, incidents, and dialogue are products of the author's and not to be construed as real. Any resemblance to actual persons, living or dead, is entirely coincidental.

Shari Parker Publishing and Printing
2785 CR 3103
New Boston, Texas 75570
903-933-6273
sharipar@yahoo.com
www.shariparkerpublishingandprinting.com

ISBN 978-0-9852685-03

10 9 8 7 6 5 4 3 2 1

Printed in the United States of America

TALES FROM MY ROCKER

CHAPTERS	PAGE

CHAPTERS   PAGE

PRANKS

A.J.

Have you ever known someone with a knack for being funny no matter what they did? A.J. was that type of fellow. Let me describe A. J. to you. He was about 6'2" and handsome. Matter of fact he had a faint resemblance to Harrison Ford. Besides having a full time job, he was a reserve deputy for the Bowie County Sheriff's Department. A.J. was a bit on the nervous side. All who worked with him said they didn't want A.J. stopping them for a traffic violation because he might drop his gun. It might go off by accident and kill someone. Besides being nervous A.J. was very forgetful. While on duty
one night as a reserve deputy, he locked his keys in the patrol car.

Everyone could tell A.J. was a ladies man right from the start. One day while the employees were working with some parts, someone put the pallet in the wrong way. The simple thing to do was take the pallet back outside with the pallet jack, turn it around, and put it in the right way.

Instead A.J. said, "Don't worry about it. I can turn it without too much trouble."

He turned the 4,000 pound pallet 90 degrees by himself just to impress this shapely attractive lady who was working with the group. For weeks after this episode his back was killing him. Another time was when a couple of young petite very pretty ladies had stopped at the building to get a coke and take a break. He started talking to one of them. It wasn't any time until his chest was sticking out trying to impress them. After a few minutes they said it was about time for them to leave, break was over. A.J. rushed out the back door and proceeded to fling open the front heavy metal doors so

3

they could see how strong and macho he was. It was amazing to see the doors stay on the hinges when he opened them with such force. When he noticed the pretty young things had already left through another door, you could see his demeanor wilt instantly as if he had been a flower that had been exposed to too much sudden heat.

A.J. had back trouble so he borrowed a friend's battery operated electric impulse device which hooked on his belt and had wires running to the spot in pain. He hooked up all the wires in all the right places. It seemed to be working just fine for him until he sat down after work and began to sweat. Soon he felt a little twinge and then another one. In just a few seconds he jumped up and started pulling his shirt out of his pants and pulling wires trying to get them loose from the battery. It was shocking him. He was jumping and hollering, "I've got to get these off before they kill me!"

The group was sitting in the work area one day talking about football.

A. J. said, "I was a punter in high school football. I had a 70-yard average."

One guy who was into sports said "A.J., punters in the NFL don't have that kind of average."

Someone spoke up and asked, "A.J. did you punt one time and it rolled 70 yards?"

All in all, what can be said about A.J. is that he was a fun guy. He was likeable, humorous, and talented in a lot of aspects. He was always willing to do more that his part.

A Real Woodsman

Jerry was as tough as a bucket of nails, but he sure had a weakness. He worked at Red River Army Depot a number of years, when he came to the Roads and Grounds Department. He was one of the good old boy types. In northeast Texas a good old boy drove a pickup truck with a gun rack and a rope hanging in the back window and had a little hay string hanging off the bed. Of course his pickup was not complete without bailing wire holding some part on. He had to wear a cowboy hat or a feed store cap, blue jeans, and work boots. A good old boy was easy to get along with, but could be riled to the point of taking care of business. Jerry had all this paraphernalia and personality to match, so he qualified as a good old boy.

Jerry would hunt anything, coon, deer, squirrels, rabbits, duck, quail and maybe even some armadillos.

I asked Jerry "Is there anything you don't hunt?" Jerry said, "Nope, there's not much I don't hunt."

He was a real hunter, a woodsman in any one's book, more like the mountain man of the old west. Besides being a hunter, he was a jack of all trades. He built his own log house, which turned out pretty nice.

He said, "Me, my two sons and buddies are going squirrel hunting and camping down on the Sulfur River this weekend."

I asked, "How far ya'll going back into the river bottoms?"

Jerry said, "Far enough that there hasn't been anyone within miles of us. We want to get where the squirrels are."

When he got back from his hunting and camping trip, he had a real story to tell.

He said, "We rode our ATVs about five miles into the river bottoms and were setting up camp when I cut my left hand bad."

He said, "I wrapped it in a towel. We rode out to our trucks, then went down to Mom's house." He got a needle and thread and sewed about a half dozen stitches in his own hand. Then they went back and camped out for the weekend like nothing had happened.

Now that's what you call tough!

He came in one day about a month later at lunch and said he had cut his hand again which wasn't much more that a scratch. He started telling about the weekend he had cut his hand on the camping trip again.

I said, "I have something that will seal that cut over real good."

It was known as liquid Band-Aid which had oil of cloves and some other stuff in it.

Jerry said, "Go ahead and put some on my cut."

I put it on the cut. After about a minute Jerry started hollering and screaming, "That stuff burns something fierce."

I knew it would burn some, but Jerry being a real tough guy and all, I thought it wouldn't be a big deal for him since he had sewn up a cut on his own hand.

He told me, "I won't be asking you for any more of that stuff." He washed it off his hand so that the burning would stop.

Some people can take the pain and some can't. No one is fond of pain. This liquid Band-Aid will set you on fire if you put it on a fresh cut. Not expecting it to hurt is enough to make a big man run and holler big time. It did Jerry. As for liquid Band-Aid, it's not a problem with some people because they have grown accustom to the burn.

Buttered

A fellow I work with related this story to me. As a four year old kid he was taking someone else's word for things that happened or would happen. Someone had told him that if you can get your head through something, you can get the rest of your body through it too. I guess four old boys always want to find out if the grass is greener on the other side of the fence. So one day as he was playing in his backyard, he thought he would give it a try since he wanted to go over to his friend's house. He wanted to go through this lady's yard that had a rod-iron fence. So he stuck his head through the fence. He found out quickly that whoever told him that your body will go through where you head goes through was wrong. He was stuck with his head through the fence and with no way of getting out. He was standing there crying and screaming and couldn't get loose. So this kind lady that lived in the house with that rod-iron fence came out to help him. She tried to get his head back through the fence but to no avail. So she went to her refrigerator, got some butter, and buttered his ears. He looked like a greased pig, but his head slipped back, and the crying and screaming was over. He didn't try putting his head through there anymore.

Cajun Coffee

We all know it's better to keep your mouth shut, set back, and watch if you're in a strange place. This fellow should have done just that. One of the jobs I held at Red River Army Depot was operating a bulldozer and front-end loader on swing shift at the steam boiler plant. Like all jobs there is some part of it you're not going to like. For me it was cleaning up the top floor where the coal and wood dust was about a foot deep. Regardless of the bad part, this was one of the better jobs I had at Red River Army Depot. After loading the conveyor with chipped wood for the boiler house, I would take the bulldozer and crush wood to be chipped up. Then I would take an hour or so break, clean up the top floor, and take a shower. This is where the good part comes in.

When the graveyard shift came on, the workers would eat popcorn, pickled eggs, summer sausage and crackers and drink ice tea every night. Plus, on Friday nights, swing shift would cook hamburgers, BBQ ribs or something along that line that was good. What more could a fellow want than to have a job like that?

Naturally, I sat around and talked to the boiler operators. They had many stories to tell of their past.

Old man King, a crotchety old man, had a humorous story to tell about the time he carried a stock trailer down into Louisiana for a salesman.

About daylight he had trouble with the pickup as he was driving into this small town in the far reaches of Cajun country.

"I'm not going to find a mechanic at this time of the morning," he thought.

He walked a little ways and saw a well-worn café in this small town. He said to himself, "I believe I will go have myself some breakfast."

He walked in and sat down on a stool at the counter.

The waitress asked him, "Would you like a cup of coffee?"

He said, "Yeah, I'd like a cup."

So she brought him a cup but only poured the cup half full.

Being the cocky person he was, he said, "Look, if I pay for a full cup of coffee, I want a full cup of coffee."

So she brought back the pot, filled it to the brim, went back, and just watched him. Once he tasted the coffee, he realized something was different about it. It was strong, bitter, and the consistency of mud.

He said, "You could practically stand a spoon straight up in it."

He also said, "I knew better than to say a word. I had to drink every drop of it or that waitress would have been back over giving me what for if I didn't."

After he finished the coffee, the waitress walked over to him and said, "Only a few people have done what you have done. What most people do here is get a half a cup of coffee and fill the rest with cream."

He finished chatting with the waitress and had another cup--half and half this time. He ordered and finished off some eggs, bacon and biscuits with gravy. After leaving the waitress a tip, old man King was on his way to finding a mechanic.

Chocolate Pie

My father-in-law was a bit deceiving just by his looks. Normally you would think of him as being a very mild mannered man. He looked like a person that would not pull a joke or prank, but he did. In fact, he was full of them.

He and I both loved chocolate pie and a good joke. One Sunday after church my new bride and I were having dinner with her mom and dad, which we did most Sundays back then.

We had already sat down at the table, finished the main course, and were about to start on the dessert when I said, "That pie sure looks good."

She had made the biggest chocolate pie I'd ever seen. It had a meringue topping that would melt in your mouth. My father-in-law had just got a big piece of it and sat down.

I hollered, pointed at the back door, and said "Look at that snake!"

He jumped up to see where it was and was ready to get something to kill it. I will always remember the look on his face when he realized that I had gotten the best of him and his pie and proceeded to eat it. Of course, there was no snake at all but I sure made it sound like there was. He fell for it hook, line, and sinker.

He said, "Oh, well," and then went and got himself another big piece of that delicious pie.

I was just doing it to him before he did it to me if he had gotten the chance. We always liked to play practical jokes on one another. Until his dying day he never did forgot or forgive me for getting his piece of that delicious chocolate pie.

Fred and Tami

We had met Fred, our future son-in-law, a few times in Tyler. He had never come home with Tami, our daughter, before. So when she came home for a visit this time she brought Fred. He is a natural comic, loves pulling practical jokes on friends and relatives. He had been pulling them on Tami all during their courtship. Well, Tami decided it was time to do some paying back on all the jokes he had pulled on her. There is a very poor neighborhood, commonly called The Row, about a mile from our home where the houses are little more than run down shacks. Tami was driving her car, so as they neared this neighborhood she slowed down and turned into one of the driveways.

She said, "Well this is it. What do you think?"

Fred was thinking and later admitted thinking to himself, "What have I got myself into?"

But then she backed out and started down the road again continuing on to our real house.

Tami had told me, "It would be a good idea if you just happen to be cleaning your shotgun when we arrive."

I told Fred, "I'm a good wing shot on ducks and quail," which used to be true.

She just wanted to make an impression him, one that would last. We did for sure. Now he is part of the family and we love him dearly. But after that, he knew he had joined into a family of practical jokers themselves.

Frog

I had just got a promotion to a new job at Red River Army Depot, and I was getting to know the people I worked with. One of them was named Wallace, but he told me that everyone called him "Frog."

I asked, "Why do they call you Frog."

He said, "It's a long story."

I told him, "I have time to listen."

Wallace retired from the Air Force to his hometown of Bossier City, La. In 1980 one of his tours of duty was in his hometown. He was stationed at Barksdale Air Force Base. His Wing Commander, who was also from Louisiana, came up with this bright idea for a recreation and morale boaster.

The commander said, "Whoever brings in the biggest bullfrog will win a $100 saving bond. Afterward everyone will have a fried frog legs and boiled crawdad feast."

Wallace was familiar with the area and knew right where to go to find the biggest bullfrogs in the world. He and his buddy went down on Black Bayou between Rodessa and Vivian, Louisiana, about 10 o'clock one night. When it was good and dark, he set out with his light and a tow sack to put frogs in. It was just right for catching bullfrogs by hand.

Let me describe Black Bayou for you. It's a long slender body of water, with Spanish moss hanging all over the trees. It would be a perfect place to make a movie. It's the gatoriest, and snakiest looking place I have ever seen. But make no mistake about it; there are fish and bullfrogs there.

Wallace said he was catching big frogs by hand left and right. Then he spied the monster of all bullfrogs. It was three to four inches between the eyes. He eased over to where it was, ever so carefully. He snuck up behind it and grabbed it behind the head. All of a sudden he found out it wasn't a bullfrog at all. It was a monster Cottonmouth Water Moccasin! Sitting in the water a bullfrog and snake's head look a lot alike. He couldn't tell which one it was. That snake was mad as all get out. As soon as Wallace picked it up and saw what it was, he put it down in a hurry. It was coming after him now! Wallace picked up a limb and started beating it as hard as he could. All the while he was backing up trying to get away from it.

He said, "I threw everything down and started running." So he outran that snake.

For sure he didn't win the prize.

He said, "I did learn a valuable lesson: Don't mess with snakes. From then on they called me "Frog".

Gases

One day, I sat down with a friend of mine, Tim. I asked him "Do you have any good stories to tell."

He said, "Yeah, I have a few."

Tim said that his dad worked at a saw mill in Oregon. Being a laid back sort of a person, it was a habit of his to take the newspaper, go into the restroom, sit on the john, and read while he smoked his pipe. After he lit his pipe, he would throw the match into the john. He had done this a thousand times in the past. After a minute or two, he smelled something burning, but he didn't really pay too much attention to it. It wasn't long, though, before he had to pay attention because his boxer underwear was on fire. He had accidentally thrown the match into his underwear instead of the john. He got the fire put out without any injuries or serious mishaps. But, he did have to go without shorts the rest of the day.

Tim also said that one time his dad was driving a huge forklift carrying a load of lumber. The fork lift rammed into a pot hole, turned over, and dumped the lumber into the office building tearing out one of the walls. Of course, they were mad, but all in all, it turned out good for Tim's dad because he was also a carpenter. He got some overtime for repairing the office wall.

After Tim telling this story, I remembered hearing about a preacher in my neck of the woods that was sitting on the john smoking a cigarette. I don't know if he threw the match in the john or if he was just smoking, but the methane gas exploded sending him flying. He broke his arm when he landed and that put him in the hospital.

We all often wondered if the Lord was trying to tell him something. If He was, the preacher didn't get the message because I heard that he continued to smoke.

Heavy Trucking

Old truck drivers like to sit around and tell stories about their past and stories they have heard. One time I was sitting at a truck stop in New Caney, Texas, and started talking to a few old timers who had been in the trucking business all their lives. One said he knew of a fellow that was badly overloaded with some heavy timbers. His gross weight was 110,000 lbs. which was 40,000 lbs. overloaded. He was going down to the Houston Ship Channel. They were going to use the timbers in the channel, and they had to be big and heavy. It was in the summer time with the temperature well over 100 degrees. No sooner had this fellow arrived at his destination than a state trooper pulled up behind him and promptly started writing a ticket. The driver knew this was going to be a big one because of the amount of overweight load. He asked the trooper how he found him so easily. The trooper said all he had to do was follow his tracks in the asphalt. With it being so hot, he had left plenty of them.

Another story, one of the truckers told was about the time he had a wide and heavy load and was going very slowly over a mountain in Oklahoma called Three Sticks on U.S. 259. The mountain was about 2,000 feet tall and was a dangerous road for truckers and everyone else. It was steep in some places where the road twisted and turned up this mountain. It was dangerous but a beautiful place to site see. It had a small town at the bottom of the north side called Big Cedar. Well, this fellow was talking on the CB radio to another trucker and asked him if he was having a hard time.

He said, "Nah, it's nothing compared to 30 years ago when I had a 1961 Emeryville International truck with a 220 horsepower Cummins engine. It had a transmission with a lot of lower gears. At that time my load weighed over 200,000 lbs."

The other truck driver asked, "How did you get it over that mountain?"

The fellow said, "One inch at a time."

New Year Eve Prank

John, Coot, and I were looking for trouble to get into. We had driven down to the Diaryette and looked at all the girls until there weren't any more to look at. There weren't any that would look at us anyway. It was New Year's Eve 1962. We had thrown a lot of cherry bombs that night--a couple into the principal's yard. He came running out in his stocking feet trying to find out who threw those loud cherry bombs. We knew that if he caught us we would find a board on the end of our tails on the next school day. He could swing a paddle pretty good. But we were long gone in that old '57 green Ford of mine. We talked to every one of our friends until everyone else had gone to find another place to park and make out or find a New Year's Eve party to go to. We parked across the street from the Chevrolet place to see who was in town. We were just plain bored. It was New Year's Eve. We wanted some excitement.

Just before midnight a small fender bender occurred on Front Street, which is the main street of DeKalb. The Bowie County Deputy Sheriff for DeKalb was there investigating the wreck. This deputy was Roscoe P. Coldtrain, Barney Fife, and a few others rolled up into one. He was about 6 feet tall and weighed in at 300 lbs. I don't remember whose idea it was, but one of us came up with the idea of what fun it would be if we would go around to the water tower, where the volunteer fire station was, and turn on the fire alarm and leave it on for a second or two. Well, when this deputy heard the fire alarm go off, he knew it was someone pulling a prank. He jumped into his car, but it wouldn't start. Boy was he mad. He pitched a walleyed-fit right there. We got out of there plenty quick because we knew someone would be coming. We finally went around on Front Street and saw that the deputy had finally gotten his car started. He was going around to the fire station to see who was there. If he had caught us, we would still be in jail. If my daddy had found out, I would have gotten the beating of my life, and I would still be grounded even though I'm 66 years old and Dad has been gone for a few years now.

If Coot's daddy had found out, all I would have said was, "It's been nice knowing you, Coot." His dad Shorty was a volunteer fireman.

I wonder if Coot and John will remember this or even own to the night that we were bored and needed some excitement. Boy, did we get excitement!

Like I have told Coot a few times; if my kids had done what I have done, I would be in jail for murder. I would have killed my kids for doing what I did. But the Good Lord is gracious, and we all have survived.

One Big Red Eye

When I worked in Facilities Division at Red River Army Depot, all the good old boys had stories to tell, especially hunting stories. One of the main contributors was Gary.

He had heard this one from someone who lived near him over in Arkansas. It was supposed to be true. This avid hunter convinced his wife to go deer hunting with him on the first day of deer season. Now she was one of the city girls that didn't know the first thing about the woods or what to expect when she got out there. It was as black as 4 o'clock in the morning could be. He took her down the pipeline clearing which had a clear vision in both directions after the break of day. He had a tree stand for her, told her to climb up there, stay put, and be real still. He continued on down to his other tree stand about a quarter of a mile away.

In about 10 minutes, she heard something coming down the same path they had come in on. The way she described it, this thing had one big red eye and was kind of noisy. It came and stood right underneath her tree stand doing only the Lord knows what. She leaned over looking at it real hard and fell out on top of it. The fight was on! She thought "I'm fighting for my life," so she was clawing, kicking, and screaming. Whatever it was ran off quickly. When her husband came up from his stand, they found out the mystery thing with one big red eye was another hunter smoking a cigar. This fellow must have been scratched up something fierce because the lady had a lot of skin under her finger nails. We all wondered how he explained all those scratches to his wife and his friends. The mysterious hunter left his deer rifle trying to get away with his life. He probably thought a wild cat had jumped on him.

If anyone recognizes himself in this story, he can go to the county courthouse and pickup his deer rifle because they turned it into the county sheriff. As far as we know no one has come to claim it. He was probably too ashamed to admit running off from a fight. If a wild cat jumped on me, I guess I would have run off too.

Pete

Pete worked at the icehouse in DeKalb, Texas, as a butcher and whatever else needed to be done as general handyman.

It was in November 1960, someone had just brought in a deer to be checked since it was a check station for the Texas Parks and Wildlife Game Warden and left it for Pete to butcher.

After the deer was checked in, Pete said to himself, "I would sure like to have some fun for once in my life."

It just so happened that someone else had brought a young yearling heifer up there to be butchered that morning also. After he butchered the calf, he cut the ears and tail off the calf and sewed them neatly on to the deer with some thin wire. The deer and calf were about the same color and size, so they were a good match.

Pete said to the next fellow that walked up to the icehouse, "John, let me show you what I killed this morning. It's a cross between a deer and a cow."

John Wilson said, "Low and behold, if it ain't! Sure looks like one. I'll go and get old George and Shorty. They ought to know more about this that me."

George and Shorty drove over to the icehouse and took a look at it. They were a little unsure of it thinking something was a lot wrong somewhere, but couldn't see where it was. For sure they didn't believe it for a second. They just looked at one another.

George said, "Pete you have a real winner there. It is different for sure."

Shorty said, "Uh-Huh, Pete you sure do," nodding his head in agreement. These two just turned and walked out laughing and talking to one another, slapping each other on the back, and shaking their heads.

Shorty said, "If that old Pete isn't something else."

This went on for a few hours. More and more people came and looked at the new found miracle and wonder of science.

Pete said to himself, "This is getting a little out of hand here. Too many people are coming and looking at the deer and believing it."

John said to Pete, "I've called the Texarkana Gazette. They want to come out to see the deer and take pictures."

Pete said in a worried voice, "You call them back right now and tell them not to come. This is getting out of hand."

John said, "What's wrong Pete, don't you want your picture in the paper and for everyone to see what has been found here?"

Pete had to start crawdading real quick and said, "John, I'm going to have to fess up. That's not an unusual deer. I cut the ears and tail off a yearling heifer this morning and sewed them on the deer. I just wanted to have some fun, but I have had all the fun I can stand. So you call that Gazette fellow back and tell him not to come."

John said reluctantly, "Oh, ok I'll do it. But I thought we really had something for real here. I wanted to be part of it."

What I have learned from this is: A little fun can get out of hand real quick, especially if it's not the truth. Pete had fun for a while, but soon the fun turned into worry.

Sand

In 1990, my dad loved to be around his good friends at the DeKalb coffee shop and carry on some practical jokes with them. One of his coffee shop buddies was Randall who owned a sand and gravel business.

My dad was about to leave the coffee shop one day and told the boys, "If ya'll see Randall, tell him I know where he can get all the free sand he wants."

Of course Randall was always looking for a bargain when it came to sand and gravel. So he called up Dad.

He said, "Mr. Charlie, someone at the coffee shop said you knew where a fellow might get some free sand."

Daddy said, "Yeah, I know where you can get some free sand, and it ought to be pretty good quality."

Randall said, "Well, how much can I get?"

Dad said, "All you want."

Randall was getting a little anxious. This was sounding pretty good. Dad knew he was buying into this joke hook, line, and sinker.

Randall asked, "Is it down at Dalby?"

"Nope, it's not down at Dalby, but it ought to be pretty good sand. You ought to be able to do just about anything you want to do with it," Dad said.

Dad didn't want to let him in on it too quick.

Randall said, "If it is too far, I can't afford to haul it, even if it is free."

Dad said, "Well, maybe you can see your way to get it. It might be a little far for you though."

Randall had to just breakdown and ask, "Charlie, where is the blankity-blank sand?"

Dad finally had to tell him by saying, "It's over in Saudi Arabia."

Randall called Dad every name in the book and a few that weren't.

He said, "I should have known better than to believe you."

My Dad doesn't get to see his old friends much anymore, but every time he sees Randall, they reminisce about the free sand deal in Saudi Arabia.

Spitting

First, let me describe the difference between country boys and city boys. City boys have a lot of friends within walking distance and have different things to entertain them like baseball or basketball since there would be more kids to play. Country boys normally only have a few boys within a mile or so. They have to find ways to entertain themselves like shooting snakes, turtles and frogs at the stock pond, fishing, riding horses, or playing catch with the baseball. If they want to see other kids they have to walk, or if allowed to, drive their dad's old farm truck. Of course, they don't have a driver's licenses and that's why country boys stay on the back country roads.

Tommy's dad's old farm pickup truck was a 1950 Chevy 5 window ½ ton pickup that was used for everything from second family vehicle, to old fishing wagon, to pulling trailers and doing farm work. This truck had seen its better days. The rubber mat in the floor had long been worn out and missing. It had dents here and there from being used so much as a farm work truck.

Tommy who was really big for his age was driving the back roads at the age of 13 only getting on the paved roads occasionally. Tommy and his first cousin Charley were going fishing on this nice early summer morning. Since it had been raining the last few days, they figured that the fishing would be good. The road to the old fishing hole was very muddy. Charley and Tommy were talking up a storm, when Charley noticed that he was getting a little something on face ever little bit. Then it would stop, and start again. He wondered if Tommy was spitting on his face. That's what it felt like to him. He didn't see him doing it, but if he wasn't doing it, where was it coming from? Then it happened again.

Charley said, "I'm getting tired of this. Tommy, are you spitting in my face?"

Tommy said, "No, I'm not spitting in your face. What do you think I am anyhow?"

Then it happened again, so Charley said, "Let's stop and see if we can figure this out before I knock the crap out of you." So they stopped and looked the truck over. Sure enough there was a very small screw hole in the floor board. Since there was no rubber mat, every time Tommy would drive through a watery mud puddle, water would shoot up through the screw hole. It was at the correct angle to hit Charley right in the face. A little detective work solved the spitting crime. Tommy took some half dried mud and put over the hole until he could get back home to fix it better.

They finally got to the fishing hole, and it must have been the right time of the day because they tore up the crappie. They ended up with enough for a good mess of fish for supper that night.

The Great Pencil Heist

In September 1952, I had just started to school in the first grade. My best friend was the elementary school principal's son named James Michael. There were 2 Mikes in the first grade at Hubbard Elementary just south of DeKalb. We sure found a way to get into trouble quickly after being in school together for only a month.

It was a week before Halloween. My parents were involved in PTA big time, and we went over to the meeting at the school on a Monday night. Being only six years old at the time, I couldn't sit still long enough to be in the meeting, so the other Mike and I were playing outside. He decided we needed to do something daring and exciting. We went into each room and stole every pencil in school except the ones where the PTA meeting was being held. The next morning everyone was mad because their pencils were gone. The principal came around asking if all of our pencils were missing also. He offered to sell everyone a pencil on credit if they didn't have the money. You could get 2 pencils for a nickel, which seems cheap compared to today. You have to remember, money wasn't as plentiful then as it is today. It wasn't long before he figured out how, when, and who did it. He made us tell where we buried all the pencils. We had taken about fifty pencils and didn't know what to do with them. We figured we would just bury them to keep someone from finding them. When I got back into class, Miss Jettie Shaver took her well-made paddle and tore my hinny up. She got both of us. At the time, I didn't think he got as much of a whipping as I did because he was the principal's son.

The worst part of this whole ordeal was waiting for my dad. I pretty well knew what he was going to do. Waiting for it was nearly as bad as getting it. When he got home and mama told him what I had done, he proceeded to take off his belt and wear me out. I told him I had gotten a spanking at school, but it didn't deter him from giving me another one. He broke his belt on me and then told my brother to give him his belt, and he used it on me. Daddy stayed mad for a long time after that because of the embarrassment to our family in the community, but Mom had a little compassion on me and wasn't mad very long.

All I have to say on this subject is that I got what I deserved, and it may have deterred me from a life of crime. Afterwards I learned that if it's not mine leave it alone. Of course like most criminals the other Mike and I blamed each other saying the other one talked them into it. Naturally, since I'm writing this story, I'm sure the other Mike is the guilty party.

The other Mike is a doctor living in Ft. Worth and has a good practice now. I had a terrible time living this down in school. Every so often, someone from school would come up and ask me what ever happened to that Lone Ranger pencil he had in the 3rh grade.

Seriously, I truly think I turned out to be better a person after the pencil heist. I learned that crime doesn't pay and you have to take responsibility for your actions good or bad.

Trucking and Whiskey

Once, while I was sitting around the office at A&T Truck Line in Ashdown, Ark., waiting for a load, Mr. Patt, the owner of the trucking company, was telling stories from his past trucking experience.

In 1947 he had a small trucking company of only 4 trucks. He had a backhaul out of Kentucky of fine Kentucky Bourbon to Dallas, Texas. He put in at a motel to get a good night's sleep which is required by law. Mr. Patt got back into his truck and made his delivery. When he got there, they found out someone had taken a brace and bit and bored a hole up through the floor and into one of the wooden oak barrels draining it of the whiskey. Apparently they just wanted one barrel or didn't have time to get more. That's all they had missing. He didn't know how someone found out that he had a load of whiskey. Either they smelled it, or they knew he had it. With that much whiskey someone had a good time getting drunk, and a whale of a hangover.

KIDS

Michael Humphries

As a Teenager in De Kalb, Texas

For teenagers in DeKalb, Texas, there was not a lot to do, so they had to make their own fun. They could go to the movies. It might be something worth seeing. But most of the time it was a rerun or a movie like Godzilla Ate New York. But the favorite thing for teenagers in DeKalb to do was to drive down to the Diaryette and sit and watch kids make out, talk to the car hops and watch their wiggly walk. It was about one mile east of town on U.S. 82. They would normally ride back and forth for a while, then finally park and watch other kids drive by to see who was dating whom and who they could talk to and shoot the breeze.

One Saturday night John and I were in town and Ben was supposed to spend the night with John. They came across John's sister, Mary, and her boyfriend Fontane. Just so happened the boyfriend had a bullhorn. It hit John all of a sudden what fun he could have with it.

John asked Fontane, Mary's boyfriend, "Can I borrow it?"

He said, "Sure give it to Mary when you get through."

He said to me, "Let's play a trick on your Mom and Dad."

I said "Nope my daddy would shoot first and ask questions later."

So he said, "We will do it to my mom and dad then!"

They drove out about midnight, parked a short distance down the road and then walked to the house.

John walked around to his mother's window where her bed was and said, "Rammy" in very soft voice. "Rammy! Wake up!"

John's mom said after it was all over, "When John was

calling my name I thought I was dreaming."

Like everyone else in the community they didn't have air conditioning. They just kept the window up and let the breeze blow through or maybe kept a huge noisy box fan on.

After a little bit they left and got behind a tree in the front yard because they were scared of what John's dad would do.

John said into the bullhorn, "Victor, come on out, it's the law, we have the house surrounded, it's no use, come on out and give up now."

The first thing that happened was the porch light came on. Out came John's mother in her nightgown and housecoat, and right behind her was his dad with a 12 gauge-pump shotgun like he needed protecting, so his wife goes out first.

They ask, "Who's out there?"

John's dad, Victor, had had a few run-ins with the law and it was running through his mom's mind, "What has Victor done now?"

After a few seconds, John and I came out from behind the tree. John's mom and dad were as mad as old wet hens, especially his dad.

Who said, "Boy I ought to beat you within an inch of your life."

But John wasn't scared because he had been threatened many times before. His dad was known to take a nip or two and you couldn't tell when he was drunk or sober. He was in a bad mood either way. But after all things settled down his mom thought it was funny for a while, until John wouldn't stop laughing about the prank he pulled on them. The boys went to bed with John still laughing.

His mom told him, "Shut up and go to sleep."

Not long ago John and I reminisced about the time they nearly got killed and it is still the funniest thing on their mind.

They learned that life is short and should enjoy it to the fullest, but also to be careful in practical jokes.

Ben, John and the 9N Ford Tractor

It seemed John and Ben didn't have to go far to find trouble, for the most part it found them. They were in their early teenage years, good old country boys in the making who enjoyed the freedom of roaming the wide-open spaces of northeast Texas.

It was a late spring morning, just after school had let out for the summer.

John came over to Ben's house asking, "What are we going to do today?"

The answer would have been different if Ben's parents had been home. They weren't. That left a wide range of choices.

John's question was answered with a question. "I don't know. What do you want to do?" Ben asked.

John said, "Let's go down and shoot snakes at your pool."

Ben said, "Nope, we are out of .22 shells. We could go and catch the horses, but you know that would take an hour or so. They are hard to catch when they don't want to be caught."

John said, "No, I'm just not in the mood to be running horses all morning. I want to go somewhere, but I just don't know where."

Ben said, "Hey, I have an idea. Why don't we ride the tractor over to Ma's house, Ben's grandmother, and get something to eat.

She always has something good." He had seen his older brother use the old 9N Ford tractor many times for transportation when a vehicle wasn't around.

They stepped out back and saw the old tractor had a plow

attached to it.

Ben said, "All we have to do is take the plow loose and we will be gone."

Ben and John both tried to a variety of ways to get the old plow off the tractor. They took the pins out of the attachment and pulled it from side to side. They didn't have much success because it weighed between three and four hundred pounds and they weighed about 120 pounds each. They took a hammer and tried to beat it off and still couldn't get it loose. Ben decided to crank up the tractor to see if moving it would help in removing the plow. He had his foot on the clutch and had twisted around trying to give John some help getting it off. All of a sudden Ben's foot slipped off the clutch. The tractor lunged forward with John on the plow. It ran through the fence, tearing it down and taking out a couple of posts. John jumped off the tractor and ran about a hundred yards. After getting the tractor stopped,

Ben said, "Come on back, John."

John said, "No you fool! I'm not riding on that thing with you ever again. I'm going home."

So John left. Then Ben noticed something drastic had happened to the tractor that he hadn't seen in all the commotion. Each wheel was bent out at a forty-five degree angle. He just stood there looking at what a disaster had taken place. Ben knew his dad was going to jail for sure and that was for murdering him.

He thought, "Well, I better fix this fence before the cows and horses get out."

That was accomplished in short order.

About that time, Robert Blankenship drove up. He was a neighbor and rancher friend of his dad. He was a very large man who always dressed neatly in western apparel. Mr. Robert, as everyone called him, wasn't a mechanic by any means, but Ben was desperate.

Ben asked him, "Mr. Robert, how about looking at this tractor and see if you can help me fix it?"

Mr. Robert walked around the old tractor for what seemed like five minutes just rubbing his chin and saying "Huh."

Ben would ask him, "What do you think?" but couldn't get a word out of him.

Finally Mr. Robert said, "Son, I just don't think me and you can do anything for this old tractor today. There's too much wrong with it."

Ben said, "How about staying around until dad gets home so you can talk to him for me? He wouldn't do anything with you around."

Mr. Robert said, "Boy, your daddy ain't going to do anything to you. He will understand."

Ben thought Mr. Robert was going to be his salvation if he couldn't help fix the tractor, but he let Ben down. Ben's heart sank to the bottom of his feet. It always seems when trouble comes the sky goes from bright and sunny to dark and cloudy. For Ben it was a dark and cloudy day.

In less than a minute, the question had gone from "What am I going to do today?" to "How am I going to get this tractor fixed before dad gets home from work?"

He spent the rest of the day trying to forget about it. He was mowing the lawn, burned the trash, repairing more fence, shelling corn for the chickens, washed dishes, sweeping and mopping the kitchen for his mom. He was hoping it would get his dad to give some reprieve for the damage to the old tractor. One of the worst feelings that a kid can have is waiting on a terrible tongue-lashing or punishment. Ben worked and waited.

Ben said to himself, "Maybe dad won't even notice it,

maybe something else will come up that will be more important, and he will have to leave as soon as he gets home."

When Ben's dad did get home, he wasn't happy about what he saw.

His dad said, "Boy isn't there anything you don't tear up? How come you did this? Just answer me that, will you?"

Ben's dad wasn't a person that would get mad and then get over it. Once he was mad he stayed mad for a long time, and it seemed like he never forgot the incidents of frustration.

Being a pretty fair mechanic, Ben's dad repaired the tractor without too much trouble. He was very relieved. He had come out with only a minor tongue-lashing, and his dad didn't have to go to jail for murdering him. As for John and Ben they continued to be best friends, and John did continue to ride with Ben and had many more good times rather than bad-just not on the 9N Ford Tractor.

Big Toe

The big question is that everyone wants to know what is running through an eighteen month old kid's mind, this one instance my granddad found out. I was the second of five grand kids and like most grandkids I always believed I was their favorite. I was always staying at Ma's, my grandmother, and Daddy Jewel's, my granddad's, house eating some of Ma's good cooking and sleeping over or just generally hanging out with them. I liked to listen to Ma's old stories, and I wanted to be just like Daddy Jewel. As time went on the other grandkids had the same privilege as I did of staying with my grandparents.

My first cousin, De Lisa, was the youngest of five grand kids. She was about a year older than my oldest son. One summer day, when De Lisa was eighteen months old, my grandmother was babysitting her. Like most two year old kids she was getting into everything. Daddy Jewel was lying on his bed with all the windows open to get a cool breeze because they didn't have air conditioning. This was a small room added on the south end of the house of about 15' by 15' with double windows on 3 sides. There were Oak trees to the south of it to make a good shade. His favorite thing to do was lay on his bed and read the paper sometimes in his undies, but not this day because he had a grandchild around.

De Lisa was bored and looking for some trouble to get into.

She said in the boldest of voices for a eighteen month old, "Jewel, I'm going to bite you."

He said, "Uh-huh" not paying her any attention at all because he was half asleep from reading the paper.

She told him again "Jewel, I'm going to bite you."

Again, he didn't pay attention to her. The next thing he knew she had bit the daylights out his left big toe almost bringing blood. He jumped up in great surprise and hollered in pain.

He asked, "Why did you do that?"

She just said "I told you I was going to bite you, and I did."

He never did get a real answer why she had bitten him.

However, he paid plenty of attention to her from then on.

I think the lesson learned here was never under estimate what a youngster will do.

Michael Humphries

Breakfast and Stuff

When I was a kid I always liked to spend the night with my grandparents, whom I called Ma and Daddy Jewel. My granddad was always up before the crack of dawn because he thought it was a sin to get up past 5 o'clock. He always thought he had something important to do like feeding livestock, getting them ready to go to the livestock auction, or giving them a shot of medicine. But the first thing he was going to do was eat breakfast. His favorite breakfast was steak and eggs with black coffee. But he didn't have steak every morning. Sometimes it would be sausage or bacon with eggs. He would pour his coffee out into his saucer to cool and then drink it out of the saucer. While he was eating his steak and eggs, and I was having oatmeal, which was one of my favorite things to have as a kid, especially at my grandparent's. They would be thick and plenty to go around. The coffee was made on the old gas range in an old coffee pot and there would always be cathead biscuits from the oven. A long with making coffee, Ma would be warming up water for shaving purposes for Daddy Jewel.

After breakfast Daddy Jewel would always shave, it never failed. My uncle would be the one to get the razor and shaving mug with a small mirror for him, because that was one of his favorite jobs to do around the house. I remember seeing Daddy Jewel put that hot wash cloth on his face for a couple of seconds and then lather up with a mug brush and then start shaving. Invariable he would nick himself but it wouldn't bleed much. He always used single edge blades. He continued to use single edge blades until his dying day.

I guess it was his way of saying he was a nonconformist. And, I'm a lot like him in that respect. If he believed in

42

something that's the way it was for him. He was a die-hard Democrat in his political views. He raised a family in the depression years, which was very hard and my grandparents had a son to die during that time period.

I was working at Lone Star Ammunition Plant with a friend of his in the early 70's.

A friend of my granddad asked me, "How did you vote?" I said, "I voted Republican."

He said, "Your granddaddy would turn over in his grave if he knew you voted that way!"

I said, "My Christian beliefs have a firm grip on my political views."

If Daddy Jewel went to town he always liked to wear a pair of starched and ironed khaki pants and a gray shirt with his best slippers and cowboy hat. That was being dressed up to him. But back in his younger days that's what all old cattlemen wore. The reason for going to town was to sit around and talk politics and solve the world's problems with the good old boys at the barbershop in DeKalb. In his younger days he would probably have taken a drink with them, but his drunken days were over by the time I had come along.

I sure wish I could go and talk to him one more time and get his wisdom from all his past years of experience in life and tell him just how much I loved him.

Cutisms

Naturally anyone that has grandkids will testify to this statement; that as grandparents we know that we should have skipped the kids and went straight to the grandkids part. You can spoil them rotten and then send them home. One time our son and his family were living with us for a month or so. They had a son about fourteen months old and he would get into more stuff that you could shake a stick at. He was Devin and the daughter was Brianna. I was sitting in the living room folding towels and washing clothes and Devin was sitting with me. I would fold one up and he would grab it and throw it away. I would then get it and put it back in the pile.

This went on for a few minutes and I put a stop to it, saying, "No, you can't do that again."

In a minute he was watching me very closely, cutting his eyes towards me to see if I was looking. Then when I wasn't looking closely he would grab it and away he would go with it. After catching him and getting it back again, he would come and set down close to me and start the game all over again.

But this time I did catch him at it and said, "You can't do that anymore."

He and I were both enjoying the game and he sure did look cute cutting his eyes towards me, but with so many people living in one house chores build quickly. So I had to get on with business.

My daughter, son-in-law and granddaughter Amie who was about two at the time, where visiting one weekend. Amie is one of the funniest kids I have seen, she enjoys eating a salad and all types of vegetables. She enjoys a video cartoon called *Veggie Tales,* especially one called Larry Boy, who is a cucumber.   My wife was making a salad and was cutting up a cucumber.

Amie said, "Oh please don't cut up Larry Boy," in a most passionate way!

She asked, "Can I hold him?"

My wife said, "Sure you can hold Larry Boy."

So she handed her the cucumber. In a minute my wife looked down and saw where Amie had eaten about half the of the cucumber.

She said, "Amie you weren't supposed to eat Larry Boy."

Amie said, "I ate his foot."

In 2005 we had our son and family staying with us again, only with another set of grandkids.

Seth our four-year old grandson at the time asked my wife,

"What are we having for supper tonight?"

She said, "I'm cooking hushpuppies and catfish."

Seth told his sister, "We were having hushpuppies and cat kittics tonight.

In 1985, one Sunday we were sitting through a series of video tapes of Dr. James Dodson at Training Union and he told this story of himself and his young son. He was playing with him at home one day when the doorbell rang, in a minute the person at the door was gone and Dr. Dodson started looking for his two year son and couldn't find him anywhere in the house. So he looked in the backyard and he saw him on the back of the tailgate of an old trailer with his legs dangling in the air. Dr. Dodson said he could hear his son saying something but couldn't quite make it out until he got closer without his son knowing he was there, he slipped up behind him and was listening.

His son was saying, "Help D boy, help D boy," in a low two-year-old child like voice.

Isn't there a time in our life's that we are like that two-year old boy?

Many times in my life I have said, "Lord help me."

J.C. Coggins

J.C. Coggins was our grade school principal at Hubbard Chapel Elementary, which is about three and half miles south of DeKalb, Texas. From the fall of 1956 until I left for high school in 1960, he was a very conscientious person. I think he really cared about how his pupils turned out in life.

He was born and raised in Lamar County, Texas.

He said to his dad one time. "I want to quit school."

His dad said you can quit, "But I will sure make you wish you hadn't."

After his dad said that he knew he had better stay right where he was because he said, "I know he would work me to death and make me wish I had stayed in school."

He just wasn't the principal of the school; he was also the seventh and eighth grade teacher. We had two grades in the same room, with each grade having half dozen or more students.

We would love to get him talking about WWII and for him to tell about all of his exploits in Europe and England. He had just graduated from East Texas State Teachers College in Commerce, Texas when the United States entered WWII. Since he had a college degree he was considered for a commissioned rank; he rose to the rank of First Lieutenant in an artillery battery. He said he went to New York State for basic training. While up there him and two more men were walking to the mess hall one morning and they weren't watching what was in front of them and one man was about to step on a rattlesnake and had his foot up and couldn't do anything but go ahead and make the step. When he did he just made it a good one and crushed the snake's head. From then on everyone looked where they stepped.

47

As Mr. Coggins was leaving New York harbor he saw the Statue of Liberty and thought to himself, "I wonder if I will ever see you again?"

They landed in England and set up camp. He said, "I never got so tired of powdered eggs in all my life."

One day a fellow from his company that was a real sweet talker with the ladies, went up to this English farm house and talked the lady out of three dozen farm fresh eggs. Everyone enjoyed having eggs for a day or two. He said one day he and another fellow officer were traveling down this narrow English road rather fast in a jeep and came up on a horse drawn hay wagon. It was too late to stop, so they got over as far as they could and all they hit was the hay that was sticking out over the wagon.

He said, "I was wondering if we were going to make it for a little bit there."

After getting over into Europe he said his platoon was held up in an old big building and a Sergeant was throwing his bayonet at the entrance door. As he threw it and it stick in the door.

A split second later the Battery Commander walked through the door and he says, "Sir, if you had opened that door a second earlier you would be dead meat."

The Commander said, "Yeah and they would be carrying you off to the Stockade for murder."

While over there I guess it was just like everywhere else. If something happens that is unusual the story gets around.

One day a British pilot was in a dogfight at 18,000 feet and his plane was hit and caught on fire. He didn't have a parachute on. It was in a compartment just to his right hand, but it was already on fire, so there wasn't for him to do but jump without a parachute.

What was going through his mind was probably, "I'm a dead man for sure."

The pilot lands in a tree covered with snow so thick that he is not hurt at all and walks away. One things for sure, Jesus had his hand on this man in the same way he does all of us. But all things don't turn so well for the next soldiers Mr. Coggins tells about.

He said a 37-millimeter antiaircraft gun crew was firing at German planes one day while a ever so slight rain was falling and the artillery fuses were so sensitive the rain set them off prematurely; killing five men.

Mr. Coggins did make it back to see the Statue of Liberty again and came home and started teaching school. In the early 50's he was Superintendent of the De Kalb Independent School District.

Lawn Chairs

In this day and time you hear a lot about latch key kids that stay at home with no one to watch them. Ben and his older brother were early day latch key kids because their parents worked and left his brother to watch over Ben. They got into all sorts of things.

Ben's parents had friends that decided to move to California, but they had too much furniture to carry, so they left a small amount with Ben's parents. They considered the stuff theirs after a few years because the friends never came to get it or ask about it.

In this furniture was a pair of heavy metal lawn chairs.

Well Ben's brother was about 12 years old and getting where he thought he was big stuff and big enough to do about anything he wanted too.

Ben's older brother said sarcastically, "I can shoot that shotgun, I have done it before."

He was suppose watch after Ben and make sure he didn't get into any trouble while his dad worked at Red River Arsenal and his mom worked at the sewing factory a Clarksville. But how much trouble can a seven-year boy get into. Naw, not much, if only given the chance he would have. But look who was getting into trouble now. His Daddy had let him shoot his 12 gauge long tom shotgun a few times and he could handle it pretty good for a kid of his age. He decided one day to see just how well he could shoot this gun. He got one of our friend's lawn chairs and set it back about thirty feet under the old sycamore tree in the backyard.

The older Brother said, "I wonder if it will even reach the chair?"

He brought it up to his shoulder and kaboom it went off,

as the smoke was clearing he could see the chair went flying end over end, Ben's brother just stood there with his jaw dropped and mouth wide open.

He kept saying "Oh my gosh! I sure didn't think it would do that."

He promptly put the gun up and he went and hid the chair in the barn cause it had knotted most of the paint off the back and it had little dents all over it. He took a hammer and tried to beat the dents out, but he couldn't.

He said to Ben, "Don't you say a word to Mama and Daddy" Ben didn't, because he knew it would be war around the house if his Daddy found out about the gun and the lawn chair.

Ben heard his parents ask in a questioning tone, "I wonder where that other lawn chair is."

After about a month his daddy found it. The older brother got a good talking too about leaving the gun alone. Even today in Ben's mind he can see that chair going end over end and his brother standing there with his mouth wide open saying, "Oh my gosh!"

When the friends moved back from California Ben dated the oldest daughter in 1963 and the two families greatly enjoyed their friendship over the years, and occasionally would run into the girls doing some shopping or running errands.

What was learned from this experience was what was already known and if Ben saw his brother getting into trouble stay back and keep his mouth shut.

Old Yellow Cat

This is very first event that I remember in my life. It was in about June 1948, when I was two. We lived about a quarter of a mile from my grandparents, on old Texas highway 26 which is U.S. 259 now. My granddad had about 30 acres of cotton like most everyone else around DeKalb, Texas, at that time. The cotton was up close to waist high. This day I had wanted to follow a big old yellow tom cat. I think, because I was trying to catch his tail which stood straight up. My grandma called Old Yellow Gut. Ma was as good as gold but she sure didn't have the gift of picking out names.

My Grandmother was the Godliest person in my life and I still miss her influence. Old Yellow Gut was going up through that cotton at about 8 o'clock in the morning which meant the dew was still on everything. As you can tell I was an adventurer right from the start. I remember going down through that cotton and didn't feel afraid at all. I was wetter than soup and the cotton plants were a lot taller than me.

One reason I wasn't afraid, I was I following a friend, that big old yellow tom cat. I felt like I knew where I was going. Mama got to looking and couldn't find me anywhere. So she called Ma asking if I was up there, which meant she hollered over the distance because we didn't have telephones in Hubbard Chapel community yet.

Back in those days, it paid to have a good set of lungs. She hollered back and said no but about that time she saw the old yellow tom cat and me right behind him. We both were soaked from head to foot with that morning dew. All I had on was a diaper and it was soaked too. She hollered back and said I was up there and all right. I think my mom probably wanted to give me a good spat on the bottom, but my grandma talked her out of it. In years ahead she would save my bottom many times over.

The Ferguson Kids

The owners of a thousand acre ranch called the B&A hired Olive Ferguson on as a ranch hand. Naturally his family moved there with him. The old house they moved into only had three small rooms and a path to the outhouse. The Ferguson family was really poor because a ranch hand doesn't make much and with ten kids it's hard to provide everything. But they were blessed. There was a lot of love in this family. After moving there is wasn't long before the B&A Ranch decided to break up partnerships. Shortly after Olive hired on they decided to dissolve partnership. They also hired a fellow out of Oklahoma by the name of Williams who had a lot of cow dogs to help the roundup. Olive and the others started gathering up the wild bremmer (Brahma) cows. When I say wild, I mean wild. When they were fed they would stand just out of sight at the edge of the brush until the person feeding them left. They probably hadn't ever seen a person up close.

They finally got part of the 350 mother cows plus calves, steers and a few bulls rounded up into a big lot. Visitors and kids that wanted to see these wild cows that were being talked about all over the country, started climbing on to the top rail of the lot fence to get a good look and spooked them. They all broke out of the lot and the hunt was on again for another month because there were wild for sure now. Some even found their way outside the ranch; they were trying to get away from all sight of man.

The ranch itself was made up of small hills and gullies. It was covered with Post Oak timber, brush and thickets just right for a cow to hide in with a minimal of pasture for them to graze on. It was divided equally by old Texas Highway 26.

Olive was small but wiry and had the temper of a wild cat. One hot and dusty day he was out hunting for these cows. For some reason he had gotten off his horse. When this twelve hundred pound wild bremmer cow jumped off this 10-foot bluff bank, he nearly landed right on top of Olive. All he had to defend himself with was the butt stock of a whip. But the butt stock of the whip was the size of a good baseball bat. She was there to get him for no apparent reason other than being mean and wild. All he could do was beat her over the head with that butt stock cause she had him penned against the bluff bank. He finally did beat her to death but it wasn't without a fight.

Olive said, "I thought I was dead for sure, all I could do was fight for my life. She was determined but so was I."

This Williams fellow was working his dogs very hard and their feet were sore, wore out and torn up something fierce with all the brush and briars. He was using turpentine to doctor their feet and kept a small can in his back pocket just in case he needed it. One day the Ferguson boys were fishing at the small lake on the ranch. They saw this Williams fellow riding his horse as fast as he could; he wasn't holding anything back, towards the lake. When he got to the lake he didn't stop he just went right on into the water horse, saddle, clothes and all. Then after he got soaked down he took that can of turpentine out of his back pocket and threw it up on the bank. What happened was the top of the turpentine can had loosened and some turpentine had splashed all over his hinny and do mean all over it. He was blistered in that area. I don't think he rode a horse for a day or two after that.

These kids had to make their own entertainment. They were always thinking up something to get into. They had set a steel trap and caught a big old buzzard. Now the decision was what to do with it. They thought on this for a day or so and finally come up with this plan. They took a dozen to fifteen corncobs and soak them in kerosene for a while and drilled a hole through the center of them. They put a wire in the corn and then tied it to the old buzzard's feet. Of course they had to take a piece of net wire or hog wire, as some people call it, with one boy on each side, to hold that buzzard down otherwise; he would have ate them up. Well, they waited until about 10 o'clock on this night in June. They lit the kerosene and let the buzzard loose and he flew straight up about a quarter of a mile, then leveled off, trying to get away from the fire and heat I guess. There was fire in the sky you could see for miles around. You could see the silhouette of the big old buzzard against the sky from the fire that was underneath him. He headed straight for the river. People were talking about this fire in the sky for months if not years to come. One lady was telling Mrs. Ferguson, the next day about what she had seen.

She said, "I know it was the Lord and He was taking His children home cause she could see His arms pulling them in." What she saw was the old buzzard flapping his wings.

Roy, one of the Ferguson Boys who is a good friend of mine, says he didn't know if it was out of respect or fear but they didn't dare tell their dad about any of the things that was pulled, not even on his dying day. He lived to be 91.

MILITARY

Alton Miller

Alton Miller was an intimidating person everywhere but one place. I worked with Alton at Red River Army Depot. He had a lot of ability, but his actions were more like that of a hotheaded teenager. You didn't dare question anything he did. He was ready to fight at the drop of a hat.

Alton carpooled with the boss since both of them lived in the same town. One day when they were coming home from work, they met what looked like Alton's four-wheel-drive hunting truck-- his pride and joy. He had been working on it for a couple of years trying to get it back into good shape.

He said, "Hey that looks like my truck!"

Sure enough it was his truck. His wife had sold it without asking him. Soon word got around that Alton might be rough and tough at work, but at home he sure wasn't the boss. The better half, which is commonly known as the lady of the house, ruled the roost in the Miller household. As far as I know, he never said a word to her about the truck. If he did, he sure didn't tell the work crew about it. At all other times Alton was never short on words about what he would or wouldn't do.

Dave's Stories

Dave was a fellow I worked with at Red River Army Depot. He had retired out of the Air Force and had a lot of funny stories to tell.

Just after boot camp Dave was stationed at an Air Force base at Minot, North Dakota. He was in an Air Police Unit while stationed there. Their job was guarding B-52 airplanes. It was unbelievably cold. They were dropped off all bundled up in their cold weather clothing at the plane they were going to guard. Then they walked around it in knee-deep snow for about 2 hours until relieved by the next guard. One kid was out there in the dead of night, scared to death. He was messing around with his M1 rifle when he accidentally fired off a round into the wing of the plane. It hit a hydraulic line and fluid started pouring out. Instead of admitting his mistake, he raked snow up and tried to cover up the fluid. Of course when they came along and found the mess, he was in deep trouble. Dave said the fellow got a court marshal and may have even gotten some time in Leavenworth prison.

While pulling guard duty there, Dave's sergeant of the guard always had a card game going with the fellows that were in for their rest. After watching for a while, Dave said to himself, "I think I can beat this fellow at cards because he doesn't seem all that sharp at it." So he got in on the next hand and tore the sergeant up at Rook. Dave soon found himself back at guard duty even though it wasn't his turn yet. The next time, he learned to lose real well. Dave said the sergeant was an old brown shoe. A brown shoe airman was one that was in the Army Air Corp prior to it becoming the Air Force. Most old brown shoe airmen were not up to the

Air Force standards. They were just hanging on until retirement.

On Dave's second tour of duty there, he was a little higher ranked, so he had more responsibilities. He said, "One experience I had was to go out on the Indian Reservation to serve warrant papers on an Indian who had joined the Air Force but had deserted and gone back to the reservation." The papers had to have the soldier's full name on them. The funny part was that the papers nearly didn't have enough room for his full name. His name was Thomas Edgar Hold My Horse While I Walk Around The Tree. I've heard that Indians name their kids after the first thing they see after giving birth. I wonder which they saw first the tree or the horse.

On this same trip to the reservation, which is mostly prairie land with very few trees, Dave saw marks in the pavement that ran for miles parallel to one another. He kept seeing signs saying "no driving on rims." He wondered what the signs and the marks meant. It wasn't long before he found out. An old car pulled out on to the highway from a gravel road with no tires at all. The tires had not only been run flat but had also been worn off the rims. The guy was just driving on the steel rims now. What a ride that must have been!

Another time, Dave had to go on the reservation with a sheriff to try to repossess a '55 Buick that an Air Force Airman who was an Indian had bought from an auto dealership but hadn't made payments on in months. When they finally found the car, the Indians had stripped the car down including taking the doors off and putting up curtains. They were using it for an outhouse. The car dealer said, "Forget it. It just isn't worth it." He couldn't get passed the smell.

At Robinson Air Force, not far from Little Rock, Dave was on patrol in the family housing area about 2 A.M. when a fellow was caught with a 20 foot extension ladder and was nowhere near his home. When asked what he was doing with a ladder at that time in the morning, the fellow replied that he was doing some household chores. There had been reports of a peeping tom in that neighborhood. They had found their peeping tom, but Dave never said what happened to this fellow. I would have to think that he had some time in the stockade.

Dave had a fellow in his unit who was an old brown shoe airman. An inspection was due on a certain day. Dave told this fellow what had to be done and wanted to make sure it was taken care of properly. He wanted the Air Police headquarters floor for his unit to be stripped and waxed to a high gloss shine.

The airman said "No problem. I'll take care of it and have it looking like a mirror by morning inspection."

Dave knew he had to keep an eye on this fellow because he was always messing up by overdoing it. So, he decided to pay a visit to the job about 9 P.M. This man had gotten such a strong solution to clean the floor that the tile was curling up at the edges. Dave told the airman to scrape up the old tile, go down to the supply to get the necessary tile and glue, and put down a new floor. It took him all night to do it, but it was completed the next morning for inspection. The airman also had to stand inspection after working all night. Dave said that the fellow just never did learn to do things the easy way.

I'm Calling You From The Jail

One of the jobs I had at Red River Army Depot was driving a dump truck. All the men had a lot of stories to tell. It was a form of entertainment for them.

One day when we were sitting around, Don said he had heard a story about a fellow from our hometown who was known to hit the bottle pretty good. The law had arrested him and taken him to jail. He called his daddy to come and get him out.

His daddy asked, "What happened son?"

Otis said, "A car pulled out in front of me from a side road real quick-like and just stopped. I hit the car from the rear."

His dad said, "Son they can't do that to you. You're not in the wrong."

Otis said, "But Daddy they have arrested me".

His dad said, "They can't do that to you son" the second time.

Otis came back and said, "Daddy, I'm calling you from the jail, and it's serious."

Come to find out the law had not arrested Otis for having a wreck but for DWI, Driving While Intoxicated.

From then on around our shop if we wanted to make a point, we would say "I'm calling you from the jail, and it's serious."

These men I worked with here were heavy into kidding and pulling practical jokes on one another. They would never forget a mistake from the past nor what was said as far back as twenty years. There was one fellow that was having marital problems and made the statement that if he ever got rid of her that he would never go back to her. This fellow left his job at Red River for some reason. He and the wife got things straightened out and got remarried. He decided a few years later to try to come back to work at Red River, but he would have had to come back to our shop. Instead of taking a good paying job and taking all the ribbing from the men from then on because they would never let him live it down, he passed up the opportunity and went on to another job somewhere else.

They kidded me about getting stuck all the time. I was stuck almost every day. I had a chain made and put in my truck so that I could be pulled out. They ribbed me plenty. Most of the time we were knee high in mud, so I think I had good reason to be stuck.

One day, I got a chance to get even with a fellow that was ribbing me so heavy. We were building a road and had to drive 26 miles one way. Low and behold, this fellow flagged me down saying he was stuck and needed me to pull him out. A log truck driver had gotten stuck, and he had tried to pull the logger out and had gotten stuck himself. We finally did get both of them out. But from then on when he mentioned me getting stuck and carrying a chain because I got stuck so often, I always reminded him I didn't go hunting log trucks to pull out.

One of the funniest things I have ever seen in my life was what someone had told me about. If a dump driver forgets to trip the tailgate handle so the material will fall out of the dump bed, the dump truck will stand up on its tailgate. One day I finally saw it happen. This fellow had driven up to a spot, failed to lower the release on the tailgate, and stood his truck on its end. This fellow asked me in a really kind way to please get in there and lower it since he didn't know how to do it. The solution was simple. All a person had to do was start the engine, put the gear shift in reverse, let out on the

64

clutch, and it would come down. I had never seen a man so scared in my life.

One day when it was almost time to go home, I was putting my drinking glass in the refrigerator. Mac was at the water keg getting a drink. He threw what he didn't drink over his shoulder. It hit me square in the back. I naturally thought he had done it on purpose. So I ran over to the water keg, picked it up, and ran towards him pushing the water valve. I was trying to wet him down like he had done to me. He ran to end of the hallway trying to get out the door, but the door was locked. He pushed so hard that he pushed his arm through the window and cut his arm something fierce.

That's what our jokes and horseplay were like at our work place. Of course our supervisor, Section Chief, Branch Chief, and on up the ladder didn't appreciate our horseplay very much.

At the end of a workday we would sit around and wait for time to go home. That is when the wild stories started. In our minds, the old break room actually held all these things that were in the stories.

We had a horse that was 9 feet tall one time. I think Howard Hughes Spruce Goose with a wingspan of 300 feet was in there, and a fellow had walked a crane off into the California coast into the ocean and out again. We told some wild tales in that break room. But for the most part it passed the time away until it was time to go home. It kept us entertained.

Kitchen Patrol (K.P.)

I joined the Oklahoma National Guard in October of 1966. It wasn't long before we had a new company commander. I guess he wanted to put the men under his command at ease and have good relations with them. We had a unit meeting in the classroom one Sunday afternoon, and he told this story about what happened to him at his first summer camp with the National Guard. He was on K.P. the first day of summer camp when the Mess Sergeant told him to mop the floors and then to roll the cut up chicken in this partially-full barrel of what he thought was flour. After mopping the floors, he got the chicken and opened the barrel. It wasn't what he thought it should be, so he asked the Mess Sergeant again if he was sure that's what he wanted him to roll it in.

He said, "Yeah, I'm sure that's what I want you to roll it in. Now get to it. Chow is supposed to be served soon."

He went back a second time and asked the Mess Sergeant again, "Are you sure?"

The Mess Sergeant was irate by this time and said, "I'm going to kick your tail if you don't get in there and roll that chicken. Time is running out."

So Private Joe went and did what he was told to do which was to roll the chicken in the barrel of ingredients. The Company Commander and the First Sergeant were the first ones to sit down and bite into the fried chicken. They nearly upchucked and were upset about their lunch. They called the Mess Sergeant and asked him to explain about the terrible taste of the fried chicken.

Then all three of them went looking for Private Joe. When they find him they started quizzing him about what he rolled the chicken in.

All three of them said, "Take us to the barrel where you rolled the chicken." Come to find out it wasn't flour at all, but floor sweep. Private Joe tried to explain but you know how it is with the low man on the totem pole. Private Joe was on K.P. for the rest of the summer camp.

Our new Company Commander said, "If you have any questions please by all means come and ask. We will try to understand what the situation is before we jump the gun."

Marine Stories

I have known and worked with a lot of Marines over the years. They all had stories to tell.

One was a guy named Johnny. He joined the United States Marines about 1974. When he got on the bus going to the reception station, he was wondering if they would have anything for them to do after they got off the bus. After he finally got there, the DIs (Drill Instructors) didn't let them sleep for three days. They had plenty for them to do.

Another fellow named Roy said that the first day in Marine Boot Camp he was given his Marine clothing. This was a red sweatshirt with a Marine Corp insignia, yellow sweatpants, and slip-on tennis shoe. Everything was too big. On the first day, when they were lined up in front of their bunks, the DIs were doing an inspection and looking them over real good. One of them grabbed Roy by the sweat shirt and stepped in front of him. With the tennis shoes being a mile too big Roy just naturally duck footed all over the place and right on top of the DI's shoes. This didn't set too well with the DI. The DI and Roy went outside to talk it over. Roy came back in with a new appreciation for the DI's shoes and not in as good of shape as when he went out. Roy said one of the recruits was sick and needed blood but had a rare blood type. Just so happened Roy had that blood type. They found out Roy had that particular blood type and asked him to go and give a pint for the fellow Marine recruit. When he finished they told him to go back to normal duties. In a few days the recruit still wasn't doing well. Roy was again asked to give a pint, and he did. They gave Roy the afternoon off afterwards. The third time came around, and they put Roy in a bed next to the fellow after giving him a pint of blood.

While going through Marine Boot Camp, part of the training was with something called Puget sticks. They were 6½ foot long round sticks with padded ends. It was really supposed to be preparation for bayonet training without the dangers of the sharpness of the bayonet. There was competition in the squad, platoon, and then within the company. Roy had won the company level. As he turned to go back to his platoon after the match, his competitor struck him from behind in the kidney area. Roy said that it hurt something fierce. The DI proceeded to pick up the Puget stick to show Roy's competitor how it felt to get beat about the whole body saying, "You don't treat a fellow Marine that way."

After Boot Camp they were ready for Artillery training at Twenty-Nine Palms, California. They traveled from Camp Pendleton, California, up to Los Angeles and spent the night there. The next morning while getting on the bus, it was kind of cool at 59 degrees. It was about a 2 or 3-hour bus ride from there to Twenty-Nine Palms Marine Corp Base. When Roy got off the bus he almost passed out from the heat. It was 120 degrees. That's quite a difference from 59 degrees to 120 degrees in one day. Roy said it was hot beyond belief.

While out in the field in the artillery training, they liked to pull jokes on one another. One fellow had a very healthy fear of snakes. They had been warned by the cadre about the Sidewinders Rattlesnakes that liked to get into your sleeping bag with you at night or would be in there when you slipped into bed. The snakes would be wet from the heavy dew that would be on them. Someone just couldn't let well enough alone. They took a lanyard off a 155 howitzer, wet it down, put it in the fellow's sleeping bag, and waited for him to climb into it. When he climbed in about midnight without checking for snakes, he felt that wet thing down on his bare legs. He came out a lot faster that he went in. He ran so far he couldn't find his way back, and they had to send a search party out hunting for him. I'll bet he never slipped into his sleeping bag again without checking it.

I worked with a lot of people over the past 40 or so years of my career. Some of the time I have had opportunities to sit around and listen to stories that these veterans of life and WWII had to tell. Walter was one of these people that had stories to tell. Walter grew up around El Dorado, Arkansas, and had worked around a sawmill prior to WWII. Anyone that worked there had to know something about work, and he was pretty muscled up from it. When the draft board called him, he went and sat before the board and recruiters that were there. A Marine Recruiter asked him if he knew anything about the Marines.

He said, "No".

The recruiter said "I think you'd fit right in with us. Why don't you give us a try?"

So Walter joined the United States Marines. He became a jarhead. They were called jarheads because the marines washed all the stuff out of your head and put back what they wanted back into it. While on board ship they got 100 replacements for the 100 that were lost in his company at Saipan. The next island was Tinian where they lost over a hundred and left the island with only 80 men. Walter was one of them. All I can say is God blessed him.

Raeford

Raeford was a crotchety, moody old man I worked with at Red River Army Depot from 1983 until 1985. This man tore up stuff and got by with it more than anyone else while saying to me, "You're not much of an operator are you?" He was already working in that department when I arrived at the job. I was soon told about all the stuff he had torn up and the accidents he'd had.

In our job we had a multitude of duties to perform, but our main job was to repair roads. One day we were repairing a road near Elliott Lake. Raeford was operating the water truck, watering down the road to keep the right amount of moisture in it. He had a young army reservist who was there for his summer camp operating the controls on the back because the controls in the cab didn't work. Raeford backed off the road to get out of the way, but he backed off at full speed into trees and brush with the reservist hollering and screaming, "Stop! Stop!" The limbs and brush were beating him up something terrible. Raeford didn't pay him any attention and kept on backing. He finally hit a tree and came to a stop with the reservist cut and scratched up something fierce. Nothing was ever was said to Raeford about the accident at all.

The next time Raeford had an accident, it just so happen to be with weekend warriors. The supervisor sent Raeford and another fellow out to pick up a D-7 Caterpillar Dozer with a twelve foot blade on it. After loading it on to the trailer the blade stuck out about an 18 inches on each side. They were of all places near the headquarters area. They were coming up to a stop sign, but the road wasn't as wide as it should have been. Some reservists were working on a

71

three quarter ton military truck with the hood up. They were hanging all over it. Here came Raeford. He didn't move over at all. He let the blade that was sticking out the side of the trailer hit the military vehicle with reservists scrambling to get off of it. He didn't stop. He just shifted gears, kept going, and said "They shouldn't been there." He left with the reservists standing there looking and scratching their heads. Nothing was ever said about that accident.

One bright sunny morning, our supervisor told Raeford to go borrow the plumbers backhoe and go dig out an area around a fire hydrant. The plumbers had just replaced a four-inch water main. The area had a lot of mud in it. Raeford began digging. About the second time Raeford put his bucket in to dig out the dirt and mud, he got hold of a pipe. Instead of letting go and getting another bite with the bucket, he started pulling on it with all the power the backhoe had.

He was saying to that pipe, "Come on up out of there you sucker." Naturally it broke. At that moment, the supervisor drove up, jumped over, and turned off the water. In less than 15 seconds we had 500 gallons of water in that hole. The supervisor just stood there and shook his head thinking, "I should have known better."

All Raeford said was, "He should have known I don't know anything about backhoes." Actually he had been around equipment all his life.

Just before Raeford retired he bought a new beautiful two-tone blue XLT Lariat F-250 Ford pickup and a large fifth wheel travel trailer. One day after coming in from the lake, Raeford was unhooking from the trailer. Since he had never had a fifth wheel trailer, he didn't know or had forgotten that you have to drop your tailgate before pulling away.

No telling how much damage he did to his new truck that he was so proud of. All in all Raeford was a good fellow. You just had to be careful around him if he was in one of his moods.

Red River Floods in the Early Days

One of my many supervisors at Red River Army Depot told me a story his dad had told him from his past.

In the early spring of 1930, a lady came to Mr. Kilpatrick, who lived at Manchester, Texas, which is north of Clarksville, saying, "Oh, please, help me get to the Oklahoma side of the Red River because my mother is dying."

The river was at its worst flood stage. With it being out and over its banks, a ferry was of little use, and there were very few bridges at that time. It was dangerous because of the whirlpools, and the logs and timber that came down it would capsize a boat. It was probably ten to twelve miles wide at the time and crossing the Red River in a wooden flat bottom boat with only paddles was a great feat. No one in their reasonable mind would consider it in this day and time. But Mr. Kilpatrick agreed to take her across.

He said, "We will have to start out at the first sign of light though."

The trip was a success; they were able to avoid all the whirlpools and timber. Just as it was getting dark they reached the other side. The lady was most grateful. I don't know if any payment was made. Back in those days money was hard to come by. Folks helped one another with what they had, and that was mostly their hard earned sweat.

My father-in-law said that when his family came to Texas from Arkansas in 1910, they crossed a frozen Red River in a wagon pulled by mules. Of course it was at normal size; which is about a quarter of mile wide. I think it would be a little too scary to try either one of those feats now. How about you?

OUTDOORS

Michael Humphries

Being a Hobo

My dad's late teenage and early twenties years were during The Depression. Being without money and very few jobs of any kind forced him and a lot of young men to do some hoboing.

I asked, "Dad, did you ever beg food at the back door of houses?"

He said, "No, I never begged food at back doors or went into hobo camps. I knew better than to hang around with them. Hobos living in a hobo camps were mean. They had to be to survive."

We had hobos come to our back door in later years. They would drink coffee out of a tin can while camping out like most hobos.

These are some of the things he told me about his roaming around over the country when he was a young man. He was riding a westbound fast freight train headed to Dallas going about seventy miles an hour. Along about Big Sandy, Texas, he wanted to get off the train and was about to jump. A more experienced hobo in the rail car with him said, "No, you better not do it. There will be a time when you can get off. But right now that jump would kill you."

My dad rode a few trains, but he hitch-hiked a ride from passing motorists more than anything else. I remember Dad telling me about walking from Omaha to Dalby Springs, Texas, late one night. There weren't very many cars that came by and those that did didn't give him a ride.

He said, "The mosquitoes nearly ate me up in the Sulfur River bottoms. I would get sleepy walking, so I would run for a while. I tried sleeping under a culvert but the mosquitoes were worst there than any place." After a twenty

77

mile trip with no ride, he finally made it to his Uncle Ben's house about daylight.

Uncle Ben was the closest person to being a parent to my dad after my grandfather died when Dad was a young teenager. Uncle Ben dropped him off at Joe Minnick's Service Station at the west end of DeKalb, Texas. Dad started hitchhiking to see his half-sister and brother at Lawton, Oklahoma. He got about a hundred miles away from home but couldn't catch a ride. He would walk awhile and then sit down awhile. When no one came by for hours on end, he just sat down and started crying.

After this little stint of hitchhiking, he didn't do a lot more of it other than asking someone he knew for a short ride nearby.

One time he was with a group of boys down in Longview, Texas. He had taken a few nips of whiskey like everyone else in the group. Someone broke a plate glass window out of a store. Everyone ran except my dad. The law was Johnny on the spot. Pretty quick. When they got there, he told them he didn't break the window. It didn't make any difference. He was one of the gang, and they said he was drunk. He received a thirty day jail sentence. Dad sent for his sister and brother-in-law to come and see him.

He asked his sister, "Hey, Sis, how about getting me out of here?"

She told her husband whom everyone called Boy, "Pay the fine. I want him out of there." So his fine was paid, but dad repaid them shortly thereafter.

After spending five days in jail he told the law, "You don't have to worry about me getting back in here. I'm going to be as honest as I can from now on. I will never touch another drop of whiskey, and I am not going to run with the wrong crowd. I've learned my lesson."

Dad's hoboing only lasted a couple of years. Then he went into what was called the CCC's.

Cowboy Jim

Jim was a good old boy if there ever was one. He took FFA in high school, liked rodeos, cows, and horses, and just about anything to do with ranching. Likeable wasn't the word to describe him. He was more than likeable. One night Jim and Tommy, who were best of buddies, went rabbit huntin' which is a favorite pastime for boys from northeast Texas. Jim had a '66 Ford pickup. Tommy was driving Jim's truck this particular night while Jim sat over in the passenger seat with a .22 rifle seated between his legs.

Jim said, "Tommy, I wonder if this thing is loaded?" He put his finger on the trigger and pushed down. The rifle was loaded. It went off shooting a hole through the roof of his Ford pickup.

One day Jim was out looking over the cows when he saw a deer among them. He eased his 30-30 rifle off the gun rack of his pickup. He took careful aim ever so easy. Kaboom! It went off. Jim had forgotten that the window was rolled up. Jim thought that his ears were never going to stop ringing.

Besides having to replace the glass in the door, he had a major case of embarrassment from having to explain what happened to the window of his pickup.

Jim and I were working together at Day & Zimmerman Army Ammunition Plant in about 1968. Our boss decided to make us walk the line.

He told us, "You can't wear your clothes under your overalls any longer."

We wondered where you were going to put your key if you locked your locker to keep someone from stealing your billfold and everything you had.

Jim asked the boss this. He told Jim, "You are going to buy the farm, if you don't keep quiet."

Jim said, "What do I need a farm for?   I have an 800 acre ranch."

It wasn't long before we found another place to work at Day & Zimmerman.

Critters

I had relatives who owned land in the wild and wooly Red River bottoms where there were all sorts of wild critters. Two of the brothers were up at their Red River bottom farm one Saturday afternoon fixing the fences and clearing the land. It was getting close to dark. Suddenly the horses became so skittish that they weren't able to control them. They started looking around in the brush to see what could be making the horses act that way. One brother had a .32 caliber pistol and the other one had a 16 gauge pump shotgun. The brother who had the pistol said to the other one, "Come up here closer to me. This pistol is not enough if something comes at me." They didn't find anything that day but in a few days one of them killed a 30 lb. bobcat. They took it to a taxidermist and had it stuffed in a fierce attack position. Every time I walked into that room it put a scare in me.

Another time they were cutting and piling brush at the old river bottom place. They heard a rattlesnake. They unpiled the brush and started looking for it. It must have been dry weather conditions otherwise they would have set the brush pile on fire. In a few minutes they found him. He was about 4 feet long. One of the brothers said he felt a little sick, but he didn't think anything about it and continued working. Later that night when he pulled off his boot, he saw where that snake had bit him on the back of the lower leg just above the boot top. The bite area didn't coagulate, and he had a pool of blood in his boot. He hadn't even noticed it. Apparently the snake had only one fang because there was only one fang mark. The only effect from the snakebite was that he got a little sick at his stomach. He said he never felt the snake bite him because while cutting piling brush you are always feeling limbs or something hitting your leg.

The morale of this story is: Take caution where you are. If your horses are spooked, there is probably a good reason.

Deer Hunting

In 1961 I began taking deer hunting seriously.

Dad said, "You need a good deer rifle if you're going to hunt. Sears has a good 30-06-bolt action on sale for $36.00."

But me being me, I said, "I have seen a British 303 with a scope for the same price in hunting magazines. I have decided that's what I want."

My dad tried to talk me out of it by saying, "Son, the Sears rifle would be a much nicer looking gun."

I thought that since this one had a scope with it that I would come out with a better deal. So, I saved up my money and sent off for it. In about 2 weeks it came in at the train depot. I was surprised it came by train. But it was here! When I pulled it out of the box, I realized Dad was right because it was an old military rifle that had a new sporterized forearm on it. The rear stock had a lot of dents and scraps and cuts from using it in WWII. It did have a scope on it, but it wasn't a deer rifle scope. It was a scope for a .22 rifle not a heavy duty one required for a deer rifle.

I said to myself, "I sure wish I had listened to Dad because I sure feel cheated."

The rifle itself it had plenty of power and would equal the 30-06 any day of the week. But it wasn't as nice looking as the Sears rifle.

A cousin had taken dad's army 03a3 military surplus 30-06 bolt action rifle that he had gotten through the NRA at Red River Army Depot to sporterized it. He put on a new stock and hand finished it to a very deep beautiful finish with TruOil. He put on a Pacmeyer kick pad, shortened the barrel down to twenty four inches, and removed the front site where it could only be used with a scope without catching on anything. He turned the bolt down so that it wouldn't catch on anything but the palm of your hand, put a good bluing job on the metal, and topped it off with a heavy duty Weaver 4X scope. When dad got it back, there hasn't ever been a finer looking gun made.

In November of that same year, Daddy had heard someone say they had seen deer on the old Branham place down close to Sulfur River. We loaded our rifles into the car and headed down there. It was a nice walk. We saw a few deer tracks but unfortunately you can't eat tracks. We came home without anything to show for our efforts.

Later that month, the same cousin who had sporterized Dad's 30-06 invited us along on a deer hunt at a Ranch close to Breckenridge, Texas. I went on that hunting trip with my dad, my cousin Denzil Jr., and his dad Denzil Sr. (whom I called Uncle Boy).

Denzil said, "Last year me and a couple of other fellows took five nice deer off this ranch."

It was about 1,000-acre ranch with some nice hills that were brushy. It looked like deer could be there. We hunted for a couple of days but no one saw a thing, except for Uncle Boy who saw a doe but didn't shoot it.

My cousin said, "I can't believe that I and the other fellows had such good luck hunting last year and none of us got any this year." We didn't come home with a thing but stories and memories of nice scenery.

For the next few years I did very little deer hunting. In 1966 I traded the British 303 for a gold watch worth about $30 then. I still have the watch and with the price of gold rising every year maybe I didn't make such a bad trade after all.

I didn't get into deer hunting again until 1969. This time I went down to Sears and bought that bolt action 30-06 for about $100. The one Daddy had always wanted me to get in the first place. It had a Mauser bolt action which is one of the best there is. It didn't look half bad to start with, but soon after all the handling the veneer finish began to come off.

I said to myself, "I believe I will try my hand at putting on a hand rubbed finish with TruOil." I would put on a coat and then hang the stock in my old Volkswagen. With all the windows rolled up in June, it was hot, and that's what it needed. In a couple of hours a coat would be dry. I put on about a dozen coats.

I said, "This didn't turn out looking too bad for the first time trying it."

In the 1972 deer season I went hunting up in Arkansas with my boss Virgil Lawton. We were up in the foothills of the Ouachita Mountains close to a community called Nathan. We got up there about midday and hunted a little bit. About dark we went to our sleeping quarters, which was an old bus body. It wasn't long before Virgil had a fire going in the old bus.

Virgil said, "Go down to the creek and get some water. We'll need some before morning." I walked down to the creek about three hundred yards away. All downhill. I didn't have a flashlight, but there was a half-moon. This didn't make for good deer hunting, but at least I could see a little bit as I brought the water back up the hill.

I was a little worried that a rattlesnake might have scurried up into that old bus and with the heat from the fire might come out and pay us a visit. If there was one he never showed up.

The next day, I found out they hunted deer in a different way from what I had hunted deer in the past. In Texas you get on a good stand near a deer scrap and wait for him to show up. In Arkansas they hunted with dogs running the deer and with people standing on paths that they thought the deer might cross. They put me at a possible spot. A deer did come out, but it was about three hundred yards from me. I only got one shot with my bolt action, and I was off aim about a mile. I had my rifle sighted in for 100 yards. I aimed high but it wasn't high enough. By then the deer was well out of range for a second shot.

At lunchtime, we went to the old country store at Nathan, Arkansas, and got some crackers, Vienna's, (or as some people call them Viennies), cheese, and a coke with a candy bar on the side for good measure. I could tell these were true country people because they had some pinto beans on a potbellied stove that they were going to have for their lunch. I like a big bowl of beans with cornbread, a healthy slice of onion, and a big glass of ice tea. I can stand this once in a while but not every day.

We didn't see any deer that afternoon. When dark came we went on the bus and spent another night camped out. On that hunting trip we went home empty handed.

One Saturday of another season we decided to scout out an area. Since it was raining cats and dogs, I thought that he wouldn't want to go. When I got there about 4 o'clock in the morning, he was ready. We couldn't go in his pickup because his windshield wipers weren't working.

Virgil said, "We need to go in your old Volkswagen."

It was 150 miles up to Nathan and back. When we get there it was about 6:30 a.m. We rode the gravel roads all day with it raining. Sometimes it rained harder than other times, but it never stopped. The creeks began to rise, but it didn't make any difference to Virgil. That afternoon I was getting a little worried because the water was getting so deep that the old Volkswagen was floating across the streams. At times the tires were spinning in the water. They would eventually catch hold on some rocks, and we would make it on across.

We were driving along and Virgil said, "Hold it. Back up a little." I did. He stepped out and spotted a spike buck. We saw a few more doe but nothing of any size.

After dark, we got lost as a goose in a hailstorm.

Virgil said, "Well, this is a pretty good spot when the season does come."

I said, "If we can find this place again that is."

We drove north until Virgil said, "I know where we are now. That's the lights of Daisy, Arkansas, across Lake Greeson."

We turned around and headed to the intersection where we figured we had taken our wrong turn. It's 150 miles round trip up to Nathan, Arkansas, plus we drove another 150 miles on gravel roads and crossing streams. I was more than a little tired at day's end from the 300 miles of traveling.

It was about 10 p.m. when we got back to Virgil's house and about midnight when I finally got into bed. I was tired and saying to myself, "I don't want to do that anymore."

I made it a point to never go hunting with Virgil again because he was taking a sip of Jack Daniels every now and then on the trip. I don't drink and I sure don't want to go hunting with someone that's drinking. I was concerned, but I didn't know about it when we started. When you are hunting with your boss, it's hard to say anything. From then on I made sure I was too busy to go deer hunting with Virgil any more. I didn't like hunting with dogs either. It didn't seem to give the deer an equal chance.

In 1974 I had just been laid off from my job at Lone Star Army Ammunition Plant. I was drawing my unemployment check and enjoying the hunting season. I had asked Loral

Earnest about hunting deer out on the back of his place. He said it would be fine.

Let me describe this place. It was about half mile off the highway across a small creek and through a thicket. The thicket looked like it would be a deer haven. The place I was going to hunt was about 30 acres with 20 huge Red Oak trees standing about 40 to 50 yards apart. They had nothing under them, but in the other areas of the field there was sage grass and nothing else. Trees and thickets surrounded the field.

I remembered hunting this place a few times before. One time I was walking from the tree stand to my car. A nice four-point buck jumped up and ran directly away and to the right of me. As I aimed my rifle at him, I could see that if I had fired that I would have shot to his left missing him all together. He was gone in a spilt second. This was the first buck that I had ever let get away from me.

About 4 o'clock on a Monday afternoon, I climbed up in the tree stand that someone had built years before. I had been there about 20 minutes when I heard dogs barking off in a the distance. It was about 100 yards in the thicket to my left. In a second the biggest buck I had ever seen in my life came bounding out. The closest neighbor's dogs had run him out of the thicket without any one giving them encouragement to do so. He was going away from me slightly to my right when I shot at him. He turned broad side to me. I shot again. He turned directly away from me. As he was running, I emptied my gun at him. He didn't go down. He just disappeared like a ghost into the sage grass. I was disgusted with myself. I went over to the area where I had my best shot at him. Low and behold, there were spots of blood as big as my hand on the oak leaves. I said to myself, "I hit him! He is down out there in that sage grass somewhere!" I tried to follow the trail of blood, but it soon ran out.

It was cloudy and about 70 degrees. I knew it would be dark soon. I thought about coming back the next morning, but at 8:30 a.m. I had to be at the employment office to file for my unemployment benefits. I was fit to be tied. I got the best shot of my life, hit at least a 10-point buck, and wasn't going to get him. I went back later the next morning, but I wasn't able to find him.

As I said previously, I don't like hunting deer with dogs. These dogs had run this deer out right in front of me just because dogs like chasing deer. No one made them do it on purpose.

Someone found my deer later. By then he was ruined and not good for anything. He was a huge 10-point buck.

The case with me is: I'm either at the right place at the wrong time, or I'm in the wrong place at the right time. When I finally get the two together, where I'm at the right place at the right time, I still don't get the deer. It kind of soured me on deer hunting.

It wasn't long before I had a job driving a semi tractor-trailer. I didn't have time anymore for hunting. In about a year and a half I got another job working at Red River Army Depot. It became apparent that I either didn't have time to hunt because I was working so much overtime, or if I had the time to hunt, I didn't have the money to buy the licenses, shells, and all the other stuff that goes along with deer hunting. I couldn't afford hunting along with all the monthly bills that were due. What it boiled down to was: If I had time, I didn't have the money. If I had money, I didn't have the time.

These days a person can't find a good public place to hunt. You have to be on a hunting lease or go somewhere else to hunt. I have always had a dream of my dad, brother, John and me going deer hunting down in south Texas where there are deer as thick as fleas on a dog. I've had the dream since John and I were best friends and growing up as neighbors. My brother doesn't hunt anymore; my dad being 91 sure doesn't hunt anymore. But I just wonder if John hunts deer anymore? I will have to ask. Maybe that dream can still come true for just me and John.

Firewood

In 1983 I was working at Red River Army Depot and had received a promotion. My wife didn't work outside the home. We had decided after our first son was born that our kids were a large investment and needed their mom at home for them. Things were a little tight. As you can imagine, it was hard to make it on one paycheck.

A fellow near where I lived had cut his timber and left some of the tops of the timber lying there. I thought this might be a way to make a little money on the side. I had been cutting firewood for myself for some time so why not cut a little for a few other people? I put an ad in the paper saying: "Firewood for sale." I started getting calls for the firewood right away. Pretty soon it was more than I could handle by myself. So my wife, son Jamie, daughter Tami, and even my six-year old son Brian came along to help. Brian to my surprise was toting wood bigger than he was. Then my son Jamie said he had some friends that would also like to help.

My wife kept criticizing me and saying "You're not making any money with paying these kids, the gas, and the wear and tear on your chain saws."

But I just kept right on cutting firewood. I simply said, "I'm enjoying what I'm doing."

A couple of men we delivered to told us something we didn't know. They had ordered a cord of wood. It took two pickup trucks to carry that much wood. When we started unloading it, they asked how much wood we had brought. I said, "A cord. That's what you ordered." They said, "The last fellow that brought us wood sure didn't bring us that much.

We don't want that much wood. You just keep the rest, and we will pay you the full amount."

They had obviously been cheated the time before.

I said, "That's not fair for you."

But they insisted by saying, "For sure we don't want any more wood. You can take the rest back with you. But, we will pay you what we owe you."

I remember selling wood to an old black couple that was very poor. When I went inside for my money I felt sorry for them. After they paid me, I went outside and then went back inside. I told them they had given me $5 too much money. They sure had a funny look on their faces. They said, "No we didn't give you too much money!" I went on down the road anyway.

One time I had delivered wood to an older couple and had to split the wood when I got it there. I was splitting it about ten feet from their house which had some louvered glass windows. I hit the wedge into the wood to split it. The wedge sprang back out and went sailing ever so slowly like it was in slow motion end over end towards those window panes. My wife and I both wanted to reach out and catch it but couldn't. It broke two of the window panes. The couple was standing there and said the same thing, "It looked like you could just reach out and catch it, it was moving so slowly." We offered to pay for them, but they said, "Don't worry about it. We have more glass panes." I sure felt bad about it. I sure didn't want it to happen.

One of my son's friends had watched me cut the wood. I guess I made it look easy.

He said, "I sure wish you would let me try cutting some. I think I can do it."

I said, "Ok, you can try it."

After he cut for a little bit, he said, "It's a lot more work than what it looks like."

He cut firewood for about a month. One day he cut his leg with the chain saw and had to have stitches. I was worried about his leg. After that we didn't cut any more firewood. That year we cut 35 cords of firewood. Some people only wanted a rick at a time while others wanted a full cord. After expenses I probably made about a $1,000. It was hard work, but it was something I enjoyed doing for a change.

Fishing with River Rats

A friend invited me on a fishing trip with a group of school officials, teachers, superintendents, principals, coaches, even janitors, their relatives and friends. The called themselves The River Rats. They all grew up in very rural areas of small farms and towns. Fishing was a major pass time to them in their younger days. These were good old country boys who wanted to return for a weekend to their roots and enjoy fishing on the river, running trotlines, and the like. This was the plan from their start in about 1980. They would meet on the last weekend in May or the first weekend in June picking a different river to fish each year. There were three rules of the camp: No rowdiness. Everyone had to get in a boat and help run the trotlines. And at the end of the camp all trash had to be picked up. Running the trotlines was the enjoyable part for me. I hadn't done it since my old friend had drowned trot lining on Lake Wright Patman in 1975.

In 1989, the River Rats met on the Trinity River near Oakwood, Texas. In 1990 it was on the Sabine River near Carthage, Texas. The next couple of years it was back to the Trinity near Oakwood and other places I can't remember.

Most of the people liked Trinity because it had a good campground and was easy to get the boats into and out of the river. One year they were on the Red River near DeKalb, Texas, but they were afraid of it because it was so treacherous with its whirlpools and quicksand. They said they wouldn't be back on it.

The old timers of the group remembered the time they had heard about the good fishing on Lake Texoma on the Oklahoma side at MaDill. They decided to give it a try. They flocked up there by the droves. They were catching catfish left and right. This one fellow said to himself, "Before I get in a boat, a game warden comes by, and gives me a ticket; I had better get a 3-day fishing license."

He went up town to a convenience store in MaDill and started talking to one of the locals there. He was telling the good success with the fish they were catching (not telling the whole story about how good it really was). In the course of their conversation, this local fellow said a catfish is considered a game fish on that particular lake.

He got out of there as quick as he could without buying any license. He went back to the camp and told the others the conversation he had with the local person. Immediately, they start packing up and getting ready to get out of there. They were not about to leave the fish. They started counting them up and putting them in ice chests. When all counting was done by midafternoon Saturday, they had 757 catfish. They all agreed if they were caught with that many they would be thrown under the jail for a long time. They said they had no idea that catfish were considered a game fish up there on Lake Texoma. They wouldn't be going back there. Everyone also agreed that someone needed to check the legal limits and size before they decided on a place to fish.

Most of the men would get to camp on Friday night, but some true diehard fishermen would get there on Wednesday. On Friday night, there would be a meal which consisted of BBQ beef ribs and the trimmings. The next morning there was a breakfast fit for a king with eggs, bacon, sausage, huge hungry man biscuits, gravy, toast, flapjacks, syrup, butter, jelly, coffee, and orange juice. All of this was cooked camp style outside by the river. Of course, by the time you got through eating a breakfast like that you didn't feel much like eating later, so lunch was leftovers from breakfast or cold cuts. About 3 o'clock in the afternoon they would start cooking the main meal of the weekend--all the fish that had been caught or what would feed this crowd. Of course, with catfish we had hushpuppies, cold slaw, french-fries, beans, sliced onion, tomato relish, tartar sauce, catsup, ice tea, coffee or water. With meals like these you could hurt yourself real easy.

At the end of the weekend on Sunday morning before leaving, everyone had to settle up and pay for the food and the group name cap after the cost was determined. With meals and the enjoyment like this it was well worth the price. I think the most people that attended the River Rats weekend fish camp were about 35. Each year they put out a newsletter telling of the upcoming event, of the past years, of places and number of fish caught, and the number of people that attended. Before leaving the remainder of the fish was divided up. My friend and I had to leave early one time, but we should have stayed. At about 8 o'clock that morning they caught a big one weighing in at better than 60 lbs.

Floods and Houses in the River Bottoms

As I promised, I'm writing this story about my in-laws house. It's a small frame house that sat down in the Red River bottoms until 1942. Until then there had been a lot of houses down there. Every year or so, the river would flood to great proportions. Everyone would have to leave, go to higher ground, and take as many possessions as possible with them. The river would flood as often as it liked until they completed a dam on the Red River which just about stopped all flooding. The spring of 1957 was one of the wettest in history for this area of northeast Texas. While they were building a dam on Lake Texoma, which is on the Red River just north of Dallas, they were also building a dam on Sulfur River near Texarkana, Texas, which was later renamed Lake Wright Patman. They said it would take 5 years to fill up. It only took the spring of 1957 to fill it bank to bank. For a long time no one lived in the river bottoms like they had in the old days of picking cotton by hand and farming with horses and mules. Then they gradually began to move back down there.

In the spring of 1990 there was another flood where the river got up to over 12 miles wide at some points. There were big snakes everywhere. Cattlemen were getting their cattle out while they were up to their bellies in water.

But there were some benefits to the floods. A friend of mine who was a river bottom farmer said that the flood had left a lot of silt on his property. He said he could tell it was rich from what he had seen. All he did was barely till it and then plant his soybeans. It made the best crop he had ever made.

My mother-in-law's house had sat down there at one time. When I went up in the attic to install some insulation, I could see that the old house was made out of very rough used pine because it still had nails sticking out of it. Some of the house had to have been well over a hundred years old. While I was up there, I could tell that the house had been on fire at one time. Some of the timber had burned to a crisp charcoal on one end. How in the world they got the fire put out I don't know because it looked like it could have been a pretty bad fire. This old house had a kitchen where the bathroom is now, but when it was moved up here on the hill in 1942 they added a lean-to to it and made it the kitchen and put a bathroom where the kitchen used to be. Along with the house that was moved up to the hill was a small building that is weathered beyond belief but otherwise in good shape. I had always thought it was just a storage house. But I was told later that it was an old cotton house.

I asked, "What is a cotton house?"

It's where people stored their cotton at the end of the day so it wouldn't get wet with dew overnight. They wouldn't have a full sack of cotton so they would put it in their cotton house until the next day. I asked my mother-in-law if any one bothered the cotton while you were gone since the cotton house had only 3 sides and a roof with no door.

She said, "No they wouldn't bother it."

Apparently there were more honest people back then than there are now. The age of this old building is unknown but if guessing I would say pretty close to a century. The old frame house and what used to be the old cotton house have weathered many storms up on the hill but haven't had to bear any floods since 1942.

Peculiar People

Bo was one of the most peculiar and funny people I ever worked with. I first met Bo in August 1981 when I transferred to a new job. Bo was working there at the time. Let me describe him to you. He was about 6 foot tall and weighed about 225 lbs. with very little fat on him. He looked like he could whip a bear, but he was as mild mannered as a little kitten. He was likeable to all and got along with everyone. In 1981 he was riding a small motorcycle to work which looked like a gorilla on a bicycle. The alternator was out on his motorcycle. Instead of having it fixed he put a car battery in an ice chest and carried it on his motorcycle. When he had to start his motorcycle, he applied the booster cables to his battery. He would rather go way out of the way to save a little than to just get it fixed. At this same time he had a part time job as a chimney sweeper. He wore a top hat to work and displayed it everywhere he went.

Besides enjoying riding motorcycles, he also liked bicycles. He got this bright idea he needed to ride it to work. Since he was working swing shift, he could ride it to work in the daylight hours starting out early in the morning. He had to be at work at 4 pm. He had to leave on his 36 mile journey at about 10 am. He forgot one thing. It was daylight when he was coming to work, but when he got off work it 12:30 am it was pitch dark. The bicycle had no lights on it. He had to ride home in the dark finally making it home about 10 am. The next morning he took off work to rest.

After working with Bo off and on for a number of years, I got to know him better. He told me he had also worked at Lone Star Army Ammunition Plant. I asked what he did over there. He said he hired in working on the maintenance crew on the railroad, but it wasn't long before he had a chance to move to another job. The job he moved to was doing field maintenance on forklifts and farm tractors which involved changing oil. I asked him how he changed oil on a forklift out in the field. He said he would lift it up with another forklift if one was available. If not, he would jack it up and then crawl under there and change the oil. I said, "Those things weigh 4,000 lbs. You are not going to get me under there. I would be afraid of that thing falling."

In later years, when I worked with him, he had put on another 100 lbs. He wasn't the most proficient person we had operating a forklift. One day, he was going to pick up a 500-gallon container of soap. He accidentally punctured the container with the forklift prong. He left the scene immediately trying to keep anyone from knowing he had damaged it. When someone asked who had caused the accident, all the witnesses knew was that it was a big white man on a little forklift. At 325 lbs. he made a forklift look little.

Rabbit Hunting

In February 1969, I was working swing shift at Lone Star Army Ammunition Plant. I had two special friends, Jim and Bob that I worked with. We all three loved to hunt together. Jim and Bob lived at Maud, Texas, and I lived in Hooks, Texas.

I had noticed for some time that there were rabbits everywhere when I came home after work about midnight. One night after work I asked Jim and Bob if they wanted to go rabbit hunting down in the Red River bottoms.

They said, "Yeah, we sure would." But everyone had to go back home to get his .22 rifle. I had told Mrs. Barkman, whose 400 acre prime Red River bottom farm my family lived on that we were going to be down in the river bottoms after work and not to be worried if she saw lights down there. We didn't want a game warden showing up. We didn't know if there was a season on rabbits or not. But we were determined to have fun trying to get some rabbits.

We got down into the river bottoms about 1 o'clock in the morning. I knew the place where there ought to be a lot of rabbits. I was right. There were rabbits everywhere. We pulled up and got out. Jim shot three like clockwork. Bam, bam, bam. Bob did the same thing. The sights on my .22 rifle were off a little bit, but I shot quite a few. One rabbit that I was shooting at never seemed to let the shooting bother him. As a matter of fact, I emptied my gun at him, and he was still hopping around. So I threw down my gun and starting chasing him.

Jim and Bob are rolling on the ground laughing at me. I liked to have never caught that rabbit. Come to find out that rabbit was full of holes where I had shot him, but he just wouldn't go down. I blamed it on the sights on my .22 rifle. In about 3 hours we had 3 dozen rabbits. If we had wanted 10 dozen rabbits all we would had to do was keep shooting. Like I said, rabbits were everywhere. That was the first and last time Jim, Bob, and I went rabbit hunting together. Jim drowned in 1975 at Lake Wright Patman. Bob was in an automobile accident on his way to work at Lone Star Steel and had his left arm crushed, but he survived to hunt again.

I will never forget the good times I had with my friends Jim and Bob and especially on that February night in 1969. I must have made a good impression on Bob and his family. One night they got a call from someone saying Mike was in jail. His two small daughters, who were about 4 and 5 years old, starting crying because they thought I was in jail. It was his cousin Mike, not me.

Ranch Hands

Across northeast Texas, there are ranches of all sizes all the way from 4 acres that a neighbor calls a ranch to the Brosecco Ranch which had a reported 45,000 acres at one time. A fellow that worked at the Brosecco Ranch during the summer vacation from high school said they shipped five thousand head of four to five hundred pound calves to market in 1963. Now you have to admit that is a lot of beef. Most people if they have land have a few cows on it. If they have a large enough herd they also have ranch hands.

A fellow quit his job saying he was going to work as a ranch hand.

I asked, "Why are you quitting a good job for what looks like a bad one?"

He said, "I want to have some fun before I'm too old."

I've never known too many people that saw any fun in starting work before daylight and getting to bed long after the sun went down. It is sometimes from can-to-can't. Sometimes the only ones you can carry on a conversation with are cows and your horse because they are the only ones you get to see. That can get mighty lonely. Very rarely have cows been known to answer back to a question, make a statement on the benefits of being a cow, or even put up an argument.

One of the most important periods of the year for a ranch hand is when cows start calving (calves being born). When it starts in late winter or early spring, a close eye has to be kept on the cows. The cows have been known to go into a very secluded place to have a troubled calving. It's just natural instinct for them to do this.

One day this fellow that was a ranch hand said, "I was helping a cow have her calf, but the little thing was dead when I delivered him."

He had to get rid of it. He took it by the back legs and swung it around and around then slung it over the fence into a gully. He started looking after the cow that had a pretty hard time with calving. In about 5 minutes, he heard the bawl of a new calf over where he threw the dead one.

He said, "Low and behold, it wasn't dead after all."

Now he had to climb down and get that tiny little thing out of the gully. The calf turned out good and healthy with no problems. A few days later as he was having coffee in the town's one and only café, he saw the town veterinarian. He told him about the ordeal with the calf which he thought was dead but came back to life. He explained that he turned around and around then he threw it over a fence.

The vet said, "Basically what you were doing was giving CPR. You just didn't know it. In turning around and around you were forcing air into the lungs, and when the calf hit the ground it gave the heart a jolt to starting it pumping."

The ranch hand said, "From then on if one wasn't breathing, I gave it the Ranch Hand Special CPR Treatment. I haven't lost but very few since then."

In Texas, most boys want to be ranch hands when they grow up. However, after seeing and hearing what they have to put with, they don't want to knock someone else out of having so much fun and will just take a regular eight to five job. My son worked on a ranch breaking two year old colts to be used as cutting horses. He has been to cutting horse competitions where old men who could barely walk would have to be helped up on a horse.

After they got up on the horse, they turned into a whole different person. The younger men couldn't beat the older men at what they know and do best.

Turkey Huntin'

In 1972 we bought a mobile home. We were so proud of it. It was nice compared to what he had been living in. We could stay cool in the summer and warm in the winter. We could do laundry right in the house where we had been carrying it to the Laundromat. We were so proud of our new home that we invited my mom, my dad, my brother and his family, and my in-laws down for Thanksgiving dinner. We had a crowd coming for dinner. Cynthia said with all the cooking and stuff that she had to do she sure wished all of us would disappear for a few hours. Being 2 years old Tami was too young to do what I had in mind. So, I said to Jamie, who was all of 4, "Let's go and see if we can find a turkey for Mom to cook for Thanksgiving dinner."

We took off into the woods behind the house. The woods were full of water. In some places we waded in water up to the ankles of our rubber boots. In other places it was up to our knees so we avoided those. I thought it would be natural to take my shotgun if we were going turkey huntin'. We walked all over those woods and saw a lot of things. We enjoyed them all. We didn't see any turkeys, but I never expected too. It was just time to enjoy getting out with my son. When the next year came around; Jamie and Tami both wanted to go. So we went turkey huntin' again.

It became a tradition for us to go turkey huntin' on Thanksgiving and give Mom some relief while she fixed dinner. On rainy mornings we would get in the pickup and drive around. When Brian, our youngest son, was old enough he came along on the Thanksgiving ritual. We kept the tradition until the kids were grown. We never got a turkey and never expected to, but we enjoyed the annual ritual. Now the grandkids beg to go turkey huntin' with Pop.

UNCLES

Michael Humphries

110

Election of 64

In 1964 my uncle was running for Commission of Precinct #3 in Bowie County Texas. Now everyone around DeKalb took their politics very serious, even at the lowest level. Uncle Billy was a real rounder and a character. He had a personality that would keep most people in stitches from laughing at the jokes and antics he pulled. But there were some people who weren't laughing at his jokes. They were the old established crowd with plenty of money. Uncle Billy was kind of known as the poor man's candidate because that's how he was raised. The moneyed crowd had their own candidate named Todd Avery. As time for the election drew near, the race got heated up. It even got to a point where there was hatred on both sides. On the day of the election there was a lot going on, like money passing hands, furniture and goods being given away for votes, and that kind of stuff on the opposing side. I don't think any money was being passed out on my uncle's side because he didn't have it.

In all of the mess, Uncle Billy was accused of election irregularities. The district attorney, who had just been elected himself in this election and wanted to make a name for himself, charged Uncle Billy with election fraud. In a short time there was a trial. Uncle Billy made the district attorney look foolish since there wasn't a good case against him. But the most hilarious thing that happened during the trial was that the district attorney got my granddad up on the witness stand and asked him if he had dressed up as a woman and tried to vote a second time at the Hodgeson Community voting place. This had the people in the courtroom rolling in laughter from the thought of my granddad being dressed up as a woman. Let's see if I can describe him. He was 6'2" in his stocking feet, weighed about 220 lbs., would have been thin if not for his beer belly, and had a hooked nose from being broken years before. He had blood vessels broken all over his face and had a raspy voice which sure couldn't be faked as a woman's voice.

My granddad asked the DA, "Do you believe anyone would believe that I could pass off as a woman from just looking at me? If they do they must have a wild imagination."

The DA was hard up for some good hard evidence. Uncle Billy was acquitted on all charges. But he didn't win the election. For years there was bad blood between the two factions. To this day if you asked some of the old timers about it, they most likely were on one side or the other.

Uncle Fred

In February 1954, I was about 8 years old and in the second grade. My grandmother's brother Uncle Fred had told her that he wanted me to come down and spend the weekend with him. I really didn't want to go, but Mama said I had to. I didn't know Uncle Fred and Aunt Zodie very well. I had only met him a couple of times at the most. But I had heard Ma talk about him. He seemed like a friendly old man, but I was scared. He was about 60 but he looked 70 because he was a heavy drinker. I asked Ma what he did for a living. She said he had farmed all his life, but he was too old to do that now. I think he received an old age pension which was money a person received when they didn't have Social Security.

It was Friday, and I left right after school was out. It was cold and windy that day. I was going to have to ride my horse down to his house which didn't hurt my feelings any because I liked to ride my old roan mare named Sop. I knew where he lived, down a long lane about a half mile off old Texas highway 26 about half way between DeKalb and Dably, Texas. The house was unpainted with a tin roof. They had firewood and stove wood cut and stacked because that's how they cooked and heated their house. They didn't have electricity; they used kerosene lamp for their light. When I got to his house, he came out to greet me, asked me to get down, and said he would put up my horse. After he came in, he introduced me to Aunt Zodie who was shy and didn't talk much. We ate supper of vegetables and cornbread. They asked me a lot of questions about school and everything, but I didn't talk much. I was shy around people I didn't know very well. It wasn't long before we went to bed. They put me

113

to bed in this dark room with a lot of covers. I was scared because I had always slept with my brother, never alone. I remember crying a little bit, but I didn't want to make them feel bad, so I tried not to.

We got up early because that's what farmers do, and he never got out of the habit. We ate bacon, eggs, and biscuits with jelly for breakfast. It rained all day Saturday. He told me if it hadn't rained we would have gone squirrel huntun'. So we sat around and talked a lot. We played checkers some, and he tried to teach me to play dominos. We checked on my horse, ate supper, and off to bed again. The second night it wasn't so bad.

The next day was Sunday, and it had stopped raining. We ate breakfast and got ready to go squirrel huntun.' When he said squirrel huntun,' I thought it was going to be the way my daddy did it with a shotgun. But he said he only had one shell and didn't want to use it. So we took his old squirrel dog and axe and walked a long way out into the woods. The dog treed one. Uncle Fred chopped the tree down and got the squirrel. The next time the dog treed again, but the squirrel was in too large of a tree to chop down. We came home with only one. We cleaned it. He said he was sorry that we didn't have better luck, but that's the best he could do. He sent that one squirrel home with me. After thinking about in later years, that squirrel was probably one of his main sources of meat. We saddled my old mare and I left. I was glad to get home to see Mama, Daddy and my brother Choice.

I came to the conclusion that Uncle Fred wasn't near as scary as I thought. I truly think he just wanted some company and someone to talk to. He was a friendly and kindly old man.

Uncle Billy

Uncle Billy was born poor on September 3, 1933, near Dalby Springs, Texas. It is nothing but a ghost town now. He grew up partly in Dalby Springs and partly in DeKalb, Texas. I remember him telling me about an incident that happened when he was twelve years old. Since his house was a good ways from the mailbox, his job was to pick up the mail after school. By providence one day, a Farmer-Stockman magazine came in the mail. It was shipped in a cover and rolled up. It was hard as a rock. After he hopped off the bus and picked up the mail, a couple of neighbor kids named Lumpkin decided he was an easy target.

One of the boys had already mouthed off, "I'm going to whip your tail."

Uncle Billy mouthed right back, "Come ahead if you think you're big enough."

The biggest one ran at him. Uncle Billy thinking fast used the Farmer-Stockman magazine as a club and whopped him upside the head. A second later the little brother jumped him. Uncle Billy wholloped him a good one too. They kept coming back again and again, but Uncle Billy had a lick for them each time they lunged at him. After a half dozen times of being introduced personally to the Farmer-Stockman, the two brothers had enough of getting lumps. They called it quits for the day, only to take up the fight later on in the schoolyard. But for that day, Uncle Billy was the champ, thanks to Farmer-Stockman magazine.

Also at about the age of twelve, Uncle Billy met his future wife. He came calling one Saturday afternoon and her daddy chased him off his property and up a tree. Uncle Billy wasn't one to be deterred. He kept coming back again and again until he finally convinced her daddy that he was all right.

In the early 1950's Uncle Billy was a good sized teenager at six foot two inches and weighing in at 165 pounds. He enjoyed sports until he came home one night with a broken nose. That was before football helmets had face guards. Two of his teammates carried him into my grandmother's house, one on each side of him. It must have done more than just break his nose because he was out cold. He also boxed when high schools were allowed to have boxing as a sport.

On Saturdays Uncle Billy had a part time job working as a sales clerk at a dry goods store in DeKalb. He brought home a large spool of twine from the store. One day I got in his old black '39 Ford car and strung that whole ball of twine round and round inside his car. I broke a lot of it trying to get out. Uncle Billy sure was mad at me for that prank.

One Halloween night he really had some fun. He and some of his buddies decided to lay out this old dressed up dummy on the side of the road with a string attached to the arm and foot to make it look like he was still alive. Naturally when someone came along and saw the 'dead man,' the driver would slide to a halt and get out to examine the 'victim'. Uncle Billy and his buddies hid nearby in the brush laughing at the good Samaritan who stopped to help that poor departed dummy.

He pulled another trick at a service station. As he innocently went to the restroom, the bloody hand of a mannequin or a bloody coat sleeve would be sticking out of the trunk. He loved the shocked reactions he got from that trick! Of course it wasn't blood at all but catsup. Apparently no one called the law because he never got into trouble.

He must have been an intimidating person in high school. Once he told a science teacher that if he didn't change his failing test grade to a passing one, he would take him outside and give him a whipping. Apparently the science teacher had no backbone because he changed the grade.

In 1952 Uncle Billy graduated and went to business school in Longview, Texas. But I think he got kicked out because he pulled so many pranks. He got a job at Lone Star Army Ammunition Plant and stayed there until he got a draft notice. He was in the army now! He spent nearly two years in Korea. In 1954, at age twenty, he married his childhood sweetheart, even though her dad had chased him away and run him up a tree when he was twelve.

After returning from the army, he started wheeling and dealing in livestock and anything else to make a dollar. Just like his dad who was my granddad. He worked for livestock barns getting farmers and ranchers to bring their livestock to their barn instead of the competitors.

In 1957, he crossed a picket line during a strike to work for Lone Star Steel. After working only a few nights, he was stopped on the way home and beat up something fierce.

Uncle Billy said, "I've had enough of that." It was back to work at what he knew best wheeling and dealing in livestock.

In 1964 he ran for Commissioner of Precinct 3 in Bowie County, Texas. It was a heated race because of the people involved. But that is another story. He ran for the office again in 1979. He even got the governor of Texas, Dolph Briscoe, to come down and campaign for him.

Uncle Billy made the remark, "Go ahead and put me in office. You know I'm a crook. Why turn someone else into one."

He ran against his first cousin but still didn't win the election. Someone remarked to me that I was going to have a relative in office regardless. I was kin to both of them. It wasn't long before the auction barn job played out, and he went to work at Lone Star Army Ammunition Plant again. Before no time he was a Stores Foreman.

One day he was standing around outside shooting the breeze. He saw a dump truck in the distance and wagered, "I'll bet that dump truck gets stuck before he gets out on the road."

The other men standing around said, "I'll take you up on that bet."

Beforehand Uncle Billy had noticed that there was a bad muddy spot the truck had to cross. No way to get around it. Sure enough, the truck got stuck bigger than Dallas. I'm sure a few dollars were exchanged on that wager.

Uncle Billy must have done something terribly wrong because he was fired from the Stores Foreman position. He landed on his feet as a Maintenance Supervisor, but it wasn't long before he was fired from that job too. His crew was loading railroad crossties onto Uncle Billy's own personal truck. But that wasn't the last straw. He was hired back in as a production worker. In no time he was Building Foreman. But he just couldn't stay out of trouble.

He messed up again, and the Line Superintendent told him, "You're through here. You'll never be back on this line."

Line Superintendents thought of themselves as little gods who could do no wrong. They thought they had total power. That was on a Friday. On Monday morning Uncle Billy was back on that line as a millwright, and the last laugh was on the Line Superintendent. He had no control over millwrights! It paid off to know someone in personnel. Uncle Billy had a strong pull there.

While Uncle Billy had this job, he was still wheeling and dealing in livestock. It wasn't long before he was back at it full time. He left Lone Star Army Ammunition Plant never to return.

In 1964, he bought the livestock auction barn in Douglasville, Texas. My granddad told me a man named Morris built the barn in 1936. It was one of the first of its kind. A large portion of it was built out of logs. Now Douglasville isn't even a wide spot in the road. At that time it had a total population of 172. One time a fellow wheeler-dealer came over to see Uncle Billy and his operation. Seeing how small the town was, he remarked, "There's not going to be anyone to show up at this wide spot in the road." The auction was always on Saturday nights. That was when it turned into a 3-ring circus. On that particular night over a thousand people came to see the auction. Some people came just to be entertained.

The fellow said, "I never would have believed it if I hadn't seen it. So many people in such a small place!"

This auction barn was a family operation. My grandmother soon decided she wanted to get in on the action. She set up a concession stand. With that many people coming, naturally she made money.

During my high school days, I remember Uncle Billy telling me he felt like he was as good as anyone on the face of the earth. "Why?" I asked. He told me he would sit down and talk to the President if he had the chance! I know he was trying to build up my confidence in myself because I was shy.

His words came true in a way. He didn't talk to the President but someone just as famous. Uncle Billy's business dealings with livestock carried him down to Miami, Florida. One day he saw Jackie Gleason and Art Carney of movie and television fame at a fancy hotel. With his 'I'm as good as anybody' attitude, he struck up a conversation with them and ended up doing business with Art Carney. Art Carney owned riding stables in New York City.

About this time Uncle Billy had two livestock auction barns; one behind his home in DeKalb and the other still in Douglasville. Before long, the auction barn in Douglasville burned which left him with only one.

On January 6, 1971, my granddad died of a heart attack. He was a big part of everyone's life, but especially my Uncle Billy's. So many people came to the funeral that it was held in the First Baptist Church of DeKalb, the largest church in town. My granddad's death left a void that couldn't be filled.

Uncle Billy bought land on Interstate 30. I asked him, "Why buy it at such a high price?"

He explained, "It will pay for itself in no time. Someone did a survey on that section of the interstate, and at any given time of the day, 600 cars passed within an hour. With that exposure, people are sure to come and see what I have for sale." He had gotten away from livestock and dealt more in farm equipment.

During an auction one Saturday night in November, 1986, Uncle Billy had chest pains and was rushed to the hospital. The following Monday he died of a second heart attack. He was fifty three years old. He had lived a hard life and had business dealings only he and a few others knew about. As with my granddad's death, it left a large void. I'm glad my grandmother, who passed away August 1, 1984, did not see him die. It would have hurt her so.

A Monday morning during the Christmas holidays in 1960 determined a lot of my character I think. I told Uncle Billy I wanted to go with him to the Clarksville Auction barn. In the meantime, my granddad planned to carry some horses to Vivian, Louisiana. I decided to go with my granddad instead even though Uncle Billy really wanted me to go with him. But deep down I really wanted to be more like my granddad, not a wheeler dealer like Uncle Billy.

Many people would say to me, "You just couldn't help but like Billy. He kept you in stitches from laughing at him."

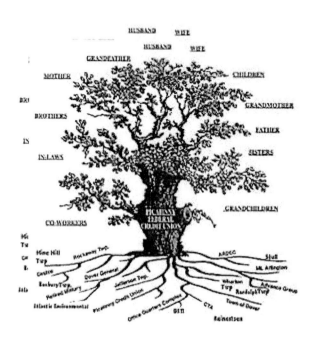

Michael Humphries

Bears and Big Cats

This story tells about what it was like in the old days of 1870 in northeast Texas.

My wife and mother-in-law related this story to me. In about 1870 my wife's great grandmother Minerva Burden Campbell and her family moved from Mississippi to a community called Box Elder, Red River County, Texas, near Sulfur River. They had bought land way back in the river bottoms because it was cheap, and no one in the south had a lot of money after the civil war. They built a log cabin since there was plenty of timber in the river bottoms. It had only 2 large rooms with a chimney for each of the rooms, a dog trot down the middle, a porch that ran the full length of the cabin, and a smaller cabin off to the side for cooking in the hot summer time. Most of the time they moved the cook stove back and forth between the summer cook cabin and the log house depending on what season it was. Otherwise, they cooked in the room which contained the kitchen area or over the fireplace.

Back in those days it was wild, all sorts of animals were in those bottoms. One day just before sundown they heard a panther calling which sounded just like a woman screaming in distress. Minerva told her two sons to get the guns and be ready to shoot when they saw the big cat come up. She positioned them on each end of the porch while she sat in a rocking chair. They had a split rail fence around the yard. She started answering the panther, and it answered her back with a scream. This kept up for about half an hour. It was beginning to get dark. They could tell it was getting closer and closer with each scream. All of a sudden it jumped up on the fence. One of the boys shot and killed it dead. They knew

125

as long as the big cat was around no one would have been safe. When it was all over they had to pry Minerva's hands from the rocking chair.

Another story related to me was when Papa Campbell came home one day and saw what he thought was a big dog near the house. He tried to get that dog to come to him but never could.

He said, "I have never seen a dog that wasn't friendly towards me."

He told his wife what he had seen.

She told him, "That was not a dog. It was a bear."

They had been seeing it off and on all morning and were waiting for him to get home so he could shoot it. After that he was a little nervous and weak kneed. We don't know if his eyesight was bad or if he had had a nip or two before he came home.

Best

One day, while my dad was in the rehab hospital following his surgery. I asked him," What was the best thing that ever happened to you?" He thought for a second and said, "It was joining the CCCs." CCC was short for Civilian Conservation Corp. It was part of President Roosevelt's New Deal plan in which he put out-of-work young men to doing public work building roads, bridges, fire towers, and planting trees. The young men had to agree to send $25 a month of their pay home to their families, and they kept $5. They had their clothing furnished and got 3 square meals a day. In this day and time that doesn't sound like much money but in the 1930s that was a great deal of money. A family could exist on that by buying just the bare basic needs.

In 1936, Dad had heard that they were talking men into joining the CCCs. He wanted to try it. They heard that Mrs. Lois Barkley, who had an office in Texarkana but lived in Simms, Texas, was enlisting young men for it. He and another man walked up to her house and asked about enlisting.

She asked his age, and he said that he was 23. "Well, you're a little too old. It's supposed to be for men from the ages 18 to 21, but I'm going to take a chance on you. Now I don't want you to let me down."

In a few days he left. He did not know where he was going. He caught a passenger train in DeKalb, Texas, going to Dallas and then changed trains. He said he didn't think that train was ever going to stop. All he knew was it was headed west. The first place it stopped was Bowie, Arizona. He got off with a lot of other young men. The camp superintendent met them and took them to camp. Some got homesick or the work was a little too hard. They left long before the 3-year enlistment was up. Usually, if they were going to leave, it was soon after they arrived.

It wasn't long before Dad was a truck driver, then an equipment operator, and then a first line supervisor over a crew. He had to go into town one morning after a snowfall. The snow covered his truck. A lot of people stopped him asking where he had come from because it was very unusual to see snow in Tucson.

He said, "Madeira Canyon. It snowed about a half foot last night."

Dad said they would work in the cooler mountains areas in the summer months and the warmer or desert area in the winter. After Bowie, Arizona, they went to Williams, Arizona, for the summer, and then it was to Madeira Canyon, Arizona, for the winter.

For the next summer, it was to Springerville, Arizona, and for the next winter it was to Apache Creek, New Mexico. That was the last place Daddy was with the CCCs. He said he wanted to go home for a little while. The CCCs tried to get him to stay by promising a promotion, but he said he would be back. Well, he met Mom while he was home and never got back to the CCCs.

He always wanted to go back to see the places where he had been. So in 1997 after I retired, he and I took a trip out there to see where he had worked. All that was left was concrete slabs of the camps and his pleasant memories of the past.

I think Dad liked being in the CCCs because he was accepted so well. The camp superintendent even let him borrow his personal car on occasion. At home he had been living with his uncle and his family since he was 16 after his father had died. He had often felt like an outcast because of

128

family conflicts.

I asked him why he thought that was the best thing that had happened to him. He said, "Before that I never had a $10 bill to my name." During the depression he had worked for 25 to 50 cents a day if he could find work at all.

President Roosevelt's new deal plan left the nation in better shape with the establishment of the CCCs. My dad was a fine example of that. Now he had skills other than hoeing, picking cotton, and manual labor. It left my Dad with a sense of self-worth and accomplishment that he hadn't had before.

Soon after coming home from the CCCs had starting a family, Dad was going from one job to another driving a truck and working as an electrician and plumber's helper.

One of his uncles that had been indignant to him in the past said, "I didn't know you could do those sorts of jobs."

My dad said "There are a lot of things I can do that you don't know about."

He volunteered for the army during WWII although he didn't have too because he had a family as a deferment. After the war, my dad got a Federal Civil Service job at Red River Arsenal. He retired as supervisor after 30 years. He had come a long way since being orphaned at the death of his dad in 1929 and working as a farmhand for his uncle.

What I learned from this is that having a skill can lead to happiness, success, and fulfillment, and it doesn't limit a person in their life's goal.

Bills

Everyone knows kids are impressionable. I guess I was too. In 1950 I was the ripe old age of four, and Mama and Daddy had jobs at Red River Arsenal. My grandmother whom I called Ma baby sat me. My granddad whom I called Daddy Jewel was a horse trader, livestock dealer, and all around buyer and seller of anything he could make a dollar on. I always enjoyed messing around with the stuff he had and seeing the saddles, ropes and all the tack that went with it. He had horses, mules, cows, sheep, hogs and even a bear. The reason I enjoyed it there so much was because there was always something to see--kind of like a three ring circus. Their house became my second home.

Daddy Jewel came home one day complaining about bills saying he was going to have to do something. On the second day he came home complaining about the same things--bills, money, and the lack of it. I was getting tired of hearing about it, and the hostile attitudes of my grandparents were getting unbearable. So, I took it upon myself to do something about it. I slipped around and got Daddy Jewel's billfold and started walking down the highway.

I was four years old and hitchhiking to town to pay some of those bills Daddy Jewel had been complaining about. I was going to start at the barbershop and from there I didn't know where I was going. The barbershop was the only place I'd been in town that was full of old men who could tell me about those bills. Of course, I had been to Ben Franklin's five and dime store to look at all the toys, but that wasn't where the bills were. I was headed to the barbershop. I thought that was a man's place where all the world's problems were solved.

I was waiting for a car to come by. The first one that passed was Woodrow Darnelle. He was my granddad's friend.

He asked, "Where are you going?"

I said, "I'm going to pay some bills for my granddad." I asked him, "Are you going to town?"

He said, "Yeah get in, I'm going to town alright."

He didn't. He took me back to the house, told my grandparents what I had done, and where I was going.

My grandmother asked me, "What in the world were you thinking?"

She promptly started telling me what all could have gone wrong.

She said, "Someone could have come along and kidnapped you and stole all the money, or a car could have run over you." She went on and on for what seemed like years. She was one that never let you forget any wrong that you had done in the past.

The only thing Daddy Jewel said was, "Boy, you better leave my billfold alone from now on."

But, at least I never heard another word about bills.

There is a lesson to be learned here and that is to never say anything around your kids that is negative because it leaves an impression.

Black Funeral

It's nice to be appreciated and honored, but I sure didn't expect it this way.

In 1990 Mickey's mother passed away, so out of respect for him I decided to go to the funeral. I knew where the church was from passing it many times between Atlanta and Turkey Huntun. In Douglasville on Texas Highway 77 there was a fairly small white frame building which might hold about 150 people comfortably. It was affiliated with the CME Denomination. I got there about 10:45 a.m. dressed in my Sunday best.

I asked a person, "Do you know where Mickey is?"

They said "No, we sure don't."

So I just went into the church building and sat down about three pews from the back. After setting down I noticed this older black lady who looked to be 100 or better but was probably only 80 from the way she was getting around. She was wondering around talking to people. In just a minute or two she made her way over to me.

As best as I could make out of her broken English she asked me, "Don't you want to move up closer to the front? "

"No ma'am I satisfied where I'm at," I said.

I tried to explain to her by saying "I'm just here out of respect for Mickey." She went on her way rambling around the building.

In about 5 minutes she was back and said in a forceful and intimating way, "You need to move up front now!"

I sure didn't want to make a scene, and I felt like if I didn't move, this older black woman was going whip up on my head.

I said, "Yes ma'am."

I got up and moved down to about the third pew from the front. She even escorted me to it. This seemed to satisfy her. In came an older white lady and her son. We were the only white people in the service of about three to four hundred. It was standing room only. In just a few minutes the funeral was under way. However, this same lady who had more or less demanded that I move down front seemed to have started her own service. She was walking up and down the aisle and talking as the younger pastor was trying to preach the service. As best as I could understand, she was praising Jesus for what He had done and what He was going to do in the future. A lot of people were asking for her to shut up and sit down, but she wouldn't do it.

Finally the older of the two pastors doing the service got up and said, "Let her say her piece for she has something to say."

She finally had her say, and after that she sat down and was quiet.

After she sat down the older pastor gave his part of the service which was very good. It was so good that I got mentally lost during his sermon and forgot about this being a funeral; I was really enjoying what he was preaching about. He spoke about Jesus and the hope that we have of what is to come and about how death is not the final event for some of us, only the beginning. We are not alone in this world for Jesus is our comforter.

I found Mickey after the service was over and told him I was sorry that his mother had passed away. I was amazed and honored that I was asked in this peculiar way to sit near the front at his mother's funeral.

I can truthfully say that I enjoyed the service for the most part although it was a funeral. Funerals are truly supposed to be times of celebration if the person that passed away was a Christian for they have gone to a far better place.

Chicken Thief

These stories were told to me by fellows I worked with and go to show what lengths people will go to keep their pride.

Troy said that as a teenager after school and weekends he worked in a small supermarket. The owner told him to watch out for a known homeless pilferer who everyone in the community called "Chicken Thief." He would steal small items like vanilla extract. For some reason the main thing he stole was Dr. Teskiners Antiseptic. There was a cat-walk at the back of the store where a person could walk across and look down each isle through a two way mirror.

Sure enough Chicken Thief came in one day, and Troy was watching him. He saw him take a bottle of Dr. Teshiners and a large mouse trap. He let him get just outside the door with the items. Troy caught up with him and told him to come on back into the store. The police had been called. They took him to the office, and the owner told Troy to stay with him until the police got there.

While sitting there Troy said, "I can understand why you wanted the Dr. Teskiners, but why did you get the mouse trap?" Chicken Thief said "I was hungry." That is a terrible thought that someone would have to go to that level to get a meal of any kind.

Another fellow told me about a time while he was in school in Illinois. On weekends he worked at the local hospital. Since he had been a medic in the army, he had plenty of experience.

One very cold Friday night with the temperature around

zero, the police brought in a homeless man whom they had found down in the rail yard in a boxcar. His toes were frost bitten. The strange thing was that he had over $400 in his pocket and had relatives in town.

Pride is a strange thing. It will make a person do horrible things even to themselves. Chicken Thief could have gone to the Salvation Army, Friendship Center, or any number of other places to get a good meal. The man with frost bitten feet could have found a homeless shelter.

Cloudcroft

I would have never believed that only a matter of feet can make a difference in weather, but I found out it can. My wife and I had carried our grandkids back to their mom in Sierra Vista, Arizona. We had traveled that same road several times and were tired of seeing the same stretch of Interstate.

So, on the return trip I said to my wife, "I'm sure tired of seeing the same old thing."

She agreed saying, "Yeah, it is boring to see it time after time."

We looked on the map. We saw that U.S. 82 ran from Georgia to Alamogordo, New Mexico. Since it ran through our hometown in northeast Texas, we decided to get off Interstate 10 at Las Cruces and travel that road.

A fellow I had worked with at Red River Army Depot had previously worked at White Sands Missile Range which was very close to Alamogordo. He told me a strange thing about a mountain just east of Alamogordo on U. S. 82. He said on the western side of the mountain it would be arid desert, and when you travel through a tunnel, the other side is lush and green with trees and grass.

I said to myself, "It might have a few trees and grass but it can't be like it is here in east Texas. It's still going to be a lot of desert even on the green side."

Before getting into the tunnel it was as desert as desert can be, but after traveling through the tunnel, it was as green as he had described it. The road kept ascending up the mountain to a height of about 8,500 feet and on top was the town of Cloudcroft, New Mexico. It was cool and inviting

137

on top of that mountain unlike the hundred degree temperature we had just left in Alamogordo. The fellow I worked with said, "The mountain is just right to catch the moisture and get a lot more rain that the lower desert area."

Apparently it got snow too because I saw signs that lead to a ski resort. We also saw a lot of real estate signs, so I figured it must have been a growing area. On the eastern side of the mountain, it was a very gradual slope. It took us about forty to fifty miles to get down to the lower desert elevation.

When I got back on the job, I called the fellow that had told me about the mountain and told him that he was right. It was a lot more than I was expecting.

I said, "It was just as green as you said it would be."

Disaster Vacation

My mother came home and told this story she had heard at work. It was supposed to have happened to a relative of someone she worked with.

A couple had just bought a nice Air Stream travel trailer and planned a trip to Colorado during the summer. The day came for them to leave. The husband drove all day the first and second day and was now tired, so he asked his wife if she would mind driving for a while.

She said, "Sure. I'll drive for a while if you want me too."

He said, "I'm going to go back into the trailer and lay down, but if a policeman stops you don't tell them I'm back there because it's illegal."

She had driven for a couple of hours when she came to a small town in Colorado. She was going a little too fast. When she came to a red light and it changed from green to red quickly, she slammed on the brakes, and the tires squealed. The Airstream Travel Trailer did not want to stop.

The husband jumped up from his deep sleep. Wearing only his boxer shorts and tank top tee shirt, he opened the door. Without thinking clearly, he ran.

"Oh my gosh! She has hit someone," he was thinking.

About that time the light turned green, and she took off. She had left him half asleep standing in the street in his underwear. He quickly came to his senses and ran down the street after her. About this time, the only two city policemen show up and take him over.

They asked, "Sir, why are running down the street in all your glory?"

He said, "I'm trying to catch my wife." He explained

what had happened and why he was in his boxer's. He also explained that he had gotten out because he thought she had had an accident at the light.

They said, "Well, get in and we'll catch her." They finally caught up to her, and asked her about her husband.

She said, "No, I don't have my husband with me." She denied it flatly and said, "He's at home." She did just as she had been told to do earlier.

They had to explain and said, "Ma'am we have your husband in the car." Then she said, "He told me to say that in case I was stopped."

The two policemen were rolling on the ground with laughter after seeing and hearing all of the explanations of the events that had unfolded.

The policemen said, "We are not going to charge you with anything. In fact since you have made our day, and it is about lunchtime, we are offering to take you to lunch."

After a fine meal at the local diner, the wife noticed her husband's fly on his pants was unzipped and motioned for him to take care of the problem ever so discreetly. He did, but in the process the tablecloth got caught in his zipper. When he got up from the table, he pulled all the dishes off onto the floor. Embarrassed wasn't the word for how they felt!

They both said, "We're going home. If this is what vacation is like, we have had enough!"

So they headed the car and RV trailer towards home.

Can you relate to this humorous situation where it would have been better to stay in bed that particular day? I think I can. But we never know what each day holds for us. Sometimes, you might as well laugh instead.

Fast Cars

My dad always thought he belonged at Daytona Beach Speedway or Indianapolis 500 because he always had in mind to get from point A to point B as fast as he could and without being caught by the law. The first car I ever remember was a '39 Chevrolet. It had been thru World War II. Any car that made it through that was pretty worn out because cars had to last back in those days. They didn't make very many cars from 1942 to 1945 because of the war effort.

The next car we had was a '47 Fleet line Chevrolet. Daddy thought he had a real car when he had that one. However, it wasn't long before he had the trading fever again. He thought he had to have a white '51 Mercury. It was pretty, and it was the fastest thing Daddy had bought so far.

By 1955 the old Mercury was worn out, so he traded it off for a brand new '55 Pontiac. In six years it was worn out, and he had the trading fever again. He bought a '57 Ford from a local dealer in DeKalb, Texas. It got great gas mileage, but it had come from Chicago where it had been through a body shop that had fixed all the many rusted spots. It wasn't long before it looked terrible. So in '63, He traded for a '61 Chevy Belair that lasted until '66. After I was married and gone, Dad started buying the more expensive cars that he could keep for a while without me wearing them out. With all the girls I was dating, I was keeping the road hot back then. He bought an Oldsmobile, 2 Buicks, and then a Ford.

My dad was always basically a Chevrolet man, and then he started buying the more expensive General Motors cars. But he never did like Fords. It's a different story with me. I can live with a good Ford as well as I can any other car.

Michael Humphries

At the age of 83, my dad took a trip to El Paso, Texas, to see his brother. He had just bought a new '96 Chevrolet Caprice. On the 800 mile trip, he got tired of traveling the Interstate. On the return trip, he wanted to go on the two lane highways that he had once traveled many years ago and see the grain fields of west Texas again. The car rode and drove like a dream, as smooth as silk. He was going along at what he thought was a pretty decent speed. He looked down at his speedometer, and it read 106 miles per hour. As smooth as the car rode, he didn't realize how fast he had gradually drifted up to that speed. He said he realized he had better slow that thing down, and he put it on cruise control at 70 miles per hour.

Daddy has had many cars in his lifetime but the one he always had at the present time was the fastest one he ever had.

Grim Hotel

It was a trip back in time, and I got a chance to experience it.

My son Brian heard that the owners of the vacant Grim Hotel in Texarkana were letting individuals go into the hotel and take articles out for a small fee. He invited me to come down on Saturday mornings and help him take the stuff out.

I wanted to enjoy some quality time with my son, so I said, "Sure. I'll come and help you."

He needed some crown molding for the house he was planning to build someday. But he also needed some bathroom sinks and a lot of tile. He was only picking up the newer sinks. But, I convinced him to take one of the original 1924 porcelain covered cast iron sinks with European handles and also a steam radiator since we both knew anything that came out of the Grim Hotel was going to be first quality.

After Brian got what he wanted, the hotel owner took us on a grand tour. It had been a grand place indeed. There was a large restaurant which served the finest of foods. There was even an outdoor café on the veranda hidden from the late afternoon sun by a wall to the west and a canopy that could be rolled down to hide the early morning sun if necessary. You could also have your meals delivered to your room if you wanted too. It also had a small shopping area, a pharmacy, a laundry, and a dry cleaning service available.

We saw how the water was heated by a huge steam boiler in the basement. The steam heat from the building's radiators were necessary to function the dry cleaners. For example, it had circular pipes surrounding it with a metal cover over them. By the time the water completed the circuit around the boiler, it was hot.

In 1924 no one knew about air conditioning, so on top of the building was a huge fan that drew air through the building. All the doors had louvers to allow air to flow. By raising the window slightly you could stay comfortably cool. There were approximately thirty rooms on each of seven floors. The eighth and top floor was a ballroom. But, what was really stunning was a multi-colored tile fountain that was the center of interest in the sitting room on the first floor. Since the hotel was only 3 blocks away from the train station, the top floor was converted from a ballroom into additional rooms to accommodate more guests mainly being WWII soldiers. I could tell they weren't the same quality as the original rooms.

Someone said the room on the northeast corner of the eighth floor was haunted. I went up there, looked around, and stood in the room for a while. But, I didn't see or feel anything weird except the wind blowing the old faded curtains around.

While most homes in 1924 didn't have electricity or running water and were heated by wood especially in the rural areas, The Grim Hotel was the show place and the classiest place in Texarkana. It not only had all the above amenities, but it was also plush and the finest quality. Anyone staying there was in the lap of luxury.

Construction was started in 1924, but something that large took more than a year to complete. One of the owners said it was patterned after the Arlington Hotel in Hot Springs, Arkansas. The same company built both of them.

Like all down town areas, Texarkana's has gone downhill and the Grim with it. But, it's beginning to find its way back to prosperity. A lot of old buildings are being turned into loft apartments. The owner we talked with said, "With the Federal Court being held only a few blocks away, the Grim Hotel will be sure to succeed." The reason we were allowed to take articles out was because they were planning to completely refurbish the hotel and restore it to its former glory. I sure want to see it restored and to visit it when it is completed. I'm sure it will be a sight to behold.

High School Football, Texas Style

A fellow I worked with named Carl told me he played high school football in Daingerfield, Texas. Daingerfield has always been a powerhouse in high school football in northeast Texas. They have had a number of kids who have gone on to play in the NFL.

Carl said they were playing Conroe in the 3A Quarterfinals in the State Playoffs in 1965. It was freezing cold on this Friday night, but at half time their coach wouldn't let them go inside to warm up. He made them stand beside a building out of the wind and stay acclimated to the frigid temperature.

The second half commenced. While the Daingerfield Tigers had stayed adjusted to the temperature and were ready to play at their best, Conroe had warmed up nicely at half time but they were about to freeze again. Carl said they wore the other team out physically and won the game easily.

The next week the Daingerfield Tigers played the Sealy Fighting Tigers in the Texas State High School Football Semi Finals playoffs. Sealy had won many State Championships before and since then. Carl said Sealy was so rough that they were putting Daingerfield's kids out of the game left and right. That year he was only a sophomore and played the defensive back position, which meant he was quick but fairly light as far as weight goes.

The Daingerfield coach told him to go in as center. Sealy had already put Daingerfield's first and second-string centers out of the game. Carl knew all he was out there for was cannon fodder, so after he centered the ball he would lay down. Of course Daingerfield was whipped up pretty bad physically and by the score also.

After graduation from Daingerfield High School, Carl played football for Kilgore Junior College as a defensive back. Apparently Carl was a pretty fair football player because Texas A&M recruited him to play defensive back for them.

Carl was also a jokester from the word go and would do anything for a laugh. He said they had one huge lineman that wasn't too bright, so he only had classes such as remedial basket weaving. The coaching staff told this huge lineman that he had to take a test in this one particular class he had. They had done everything they could do to keep him passing. They told him they had the answers to the questions, but he had to take the test himself. It being a multiple choice they thought it would be a shoe-in for an A on the test.

Well, guess what happened? He failed the test and said, "Coach I didn't know where the answers went to which questions."

Carl had a good time ribbing this fellow about failing the test when he had the answers. He said "This fellow looked like a gorilla and acted even more like one."

Carl wasn't too far away from being at the bottom of the pile in brightness himself.

I asked him, "What courses did you take at Texas A&M?"

He said, "Industrial Education. It was as easy as I could get and still graduate."

In 1984, Daingerfield High School was playing Medina Valley for the 3A State Championship in football at Baylor Stadium at Waco.

My supervisor at Red River Army Depot said, "Medina Valley doesn't even belong in the playoffs. They just have fourteen kids suited out on the whole team. They only got in the State Championship game by pure luck."

I said, "No, you don't get that far if you don't have some skill and talent."

Now I wasn't necessarily pulling against Daingerfield so much. I just wanted to shut the mouth of this big-mouth and know-it-all supervisor. So I was rooting for Medina Valley.

The Saturday night of the game, I rigged up a contraption with my old television antenna to my radio. I was surprised to pick up the game on it. The radio commentator seemed to have the same opinion as my supervisor in the fact that Medina Valley had only 14 kids suited up to play. That meant most of those kids had to play both offense and defense, and if they had many injuries they were sunk. Of course the commentator was from Daingerfield so what could you expect?

As the game started both teams were playing flawless football. Daingerfield scored first, but Medina Valley came right back and scored. At half-time the score was tied at seven all. On the opening kickoff at the beginning of the second half, a Medina Valley kid took it all the way from about the ten-yard line to Daingerfield's end zone without being touched. That kind of took the wind out of Daingerfield's sail. The rest of the game was just nip and tuck, but Medina Valley came out on top with a score of 21 to 13.

On the following Monday morning, I had to get my ribbing in on the know-it-all supervisor.

I said, "Medina Valley doesn't even belong in the playoffs do they, Bill?"

Of course from then on I wasn't his favorite employee.

I heard a year or so later about a kid named Copalander who was playing Quarterback for Rice University. That just happened to be the name of the kid that had played quarterback for Medina Valley. Apparently he had a lot of skill and talent just like I said about the whole Medina Valley team.

Houston, Texas

I have a lot of memories of being a kid, and most of them are good. But this is not one of them.

It's funny now, but then it wasn't. In 1953 my mom lost her job at Red River Arsenal, and my dad thought he was going to lose his job also. So my parents thought it would be wise for my mom to go to Houston, Texas, get a job, and set up housekeeping so that when my dad got down there things wouldn't be such a hassle. We had relatives there, and they told my mom that there were a lot of jobs.

My mom, brother, and I moved to Houston on a bright clear day. That was the last time it was bright and clear for me. We moved into a 2-bedroom upstairs apartment with a bathroom that we had to share with a family on the other end of the building. The move was into an apartment with my mom's first cousin who was more like a sister to her and an aunt to me. They lived just off Picket Street, a major thoroughfare in downtown Houston. The apartment was clean and didn't have a smell, but six people living in that small upstairs apartment sure wasn't the best arrangement. Their son, Daryl, who was about 3 years old at the time, slept with his mom and dad. I had to sleep in his baby bed. All I remember was it was uncomfortable. Mom told me I would like it and I believed her. She was hoping. Boy was she ever wrong.

My brother did well for the most part, but for me it was like a fish out of water. I was seven years old, and all I had ever known was the country life. I always had a horse to ride, and plenty of open space to roam. Hubbard Chapel Elementary only had about 60 kids with 2 grades in each room with one teacher per room. It went to the eighth grade.

All the kids were friends or at least knew one another. It had grass and trees to climb with the kids playing all sorts of games.

One of the first things we had to get use to was the sound of the city with all of it hustle and bustle. The main thing that kept me awake at night was about every five minutes the sound of sirens. Ambulances, fire trucks and police cars were always roaring by.

I realized as soon as I got there that I was in the wrong place. The teacher was gruff and no kids wanted to be my friend. The schoolyard at John Morrow Elementary had an 8 foot high chain link fence around it, no trees, no grass, only pea gravel in the schoolyard. To me it looked more like a prison than a school.

My mom let me off one morning at the school gate. I let her get out of sight, and I headed home. She met me at the corner and asked me where I was going. I said I was sick and was going home. She turned me around and sent me back to school. I was sick alright, but it was homesick beyond belief. I remember I had to walk to get home. I had to cross a busy 4-lane street. I was scared to walk across by myself. So sometimes I would try to wait until someone would come along and walk with them. But when I did that, they looked at me funny. So I didn't do much of that either. A lot of the time, I would wait on my brother who was 5 years older than I was. Sometimes I would walk over to his school which was John Daly Junior High. He enjoyed his little stint. He was already a member of the crossing guard at his school.

One time I was at his school waiting for him. An older lady wanted me come see her. She motioned for me to come over to her house. She was a kindly old person, but I was scared. She gave me an apple. I thanked her in a shy way and was out of there.

The only thing I can remember that I enjoyed was the Howdy Doody Show on TV, but The Buster Brown Theater was my favorite. Both came on Saturday morning. They were good. I remember watching wrestling. I thought it was real. We didn't have a television of our own until about a year after we got back home.

One Sunday afternoon Uncle Bill and Aunt Re took us to see the San Jacinto Battlefield Monument and the Battleship Texas. Anything to keep us occupied, especially me, since mom worked on weekends.

After about 2 months my dad came down to spend the weekend with us. He said he didn't think he was going to lose his job after all. So Monday morning mom turned in her resignation at the hospital where she worked as a cashier. She had a good job and didn't want to give it up because it paid good money. But money couldn't cure the problem with me. A few times my grandmother tried to lay a guilt trip on me saying I was the problem. So my mom had to leave Houston and give up that good job.

One of the few pleasant things I remember about Houston was that the temperature was always warm and it rained very little.

When we got home, the first place we went was to see my grandparents. After I got back into school at Hubbard for about 2 or 3 weeks I really was overly excited about being home. My teacher Mrs. Jettie Stuart sat me down one day and asked me, "What is the problem with you? You are a wild person!" I said, "I'm just happy to be home." To me, it was like getting out of jail.

How I Met My Cynthia

It was my second year at Texarkana College, and I had a job driving a college bus. It paid a dollar a day and meals. I guess the bus was supposed to get more students to attend college, and we had about 20 people riding regular and more from time to time.

On the first day I stopped for anyone that was out beside the road. Of course I didn't pick up anyone that wasn't going to college. We sure had a full load that first morning. I started off south of De Kalb, and then stopped at New Boston, then in Hooks, and a few other places along the way to the college. I got to greet and admire all the young ladies as they got on. I really enjoyed that.

At Hooks I had just one stop, and I remember it well. This small girl with short curly red hair and wearing white cat eye glasses was waiting beside US 82. She was short and had a hard time getting up the bus steps with all the books she had in her hands and with a tight skirt on also. She had on a yellow suit type of outfit. I have to admit she was striking and had a figure to go with all that appearance although she only weighed about 90 lbs.

Later on she told me that when she first saw me that she made the remark to herself, "I don't know it, and he doesn't know it, but I'm going to marry that old boy someday."

One afternoon on the way home, I was supposed to let her off. I forget to stop, and the other girls wouldn't let her come up the front.

I went about 200 yards before someone said, "You need to let Cynthia off." She said Martha had held her back to see if I would remember. If she had been up front I wouldn't have forgotten about her. Later she said that I was probably

153

thinking about some "blame blonde." It wasn't long before I forgot her again, only it was in the morning this time. She was on the side of the road waiting, and I passed her up. My good friend Ronnie was sitting just behind me and was talking to me so I wasn't paying attention. She had to go and call her Aunt Lois to come and take her to college. I met her in the hall where our lockers were and said I was sorry about leaving her. I gave the excuse that she was hiding behind the sign post.

She said to herself, "He was thinking about those blame blondes again. I know I'm thin but not that thin." She said she would have liked to hit me, but she just smiled and said that it was alright.

I really had a problem at college. I just couldn't settle down to one girl. My boss that was over the college buses had a comment about me. He said "Mike, you are like the dew covering the south. I see you everywhere on campus and with a different girl each time."

It was the middle of March, and it was my habit to go up on the second floor of the student center to see who I could see. Sometimes Cynthia was there and sometimes she wasn't. Just so happened she was there this time. I sat down, and we started a conversation. Before I knew it, I had asked her out for a date on Friday March 19th. But there was a problem. I had already asked Sharon out for Saturday night of the 20th. So I said it would have to be on a Friday night, and after that we had a date on Sunday afternoon. She said she thought I wasn't going to ask her out and that she had been waiting all year. I said I saved the best until last. But after that Sunday, it's all been Cynthia.

She said she and Sharon had a talk, but she would never tell what was said. The thing that attracted me to her besides the short curly red hair was she was full of life, smart,

154

always had a smile on her face, and always had a positive attitude.

One day after about 3 years of marriage, I mentioned Sharon's name. My wife threw something and hit me in a very sensitive spot.

She said, "That will teach you to mention her name again."

I was the only person Cynthia dated in all of her life. When she told her mom and dad that she had a date while they were at the supper table, her grandmother spoke up and said, "That's the one she's going to marry."

All of this happened in the school year of '65 and '66. We were married on December 23, 1966. I can truly say I have never regretted getting hitched up to that pretty red head. We now have three kids, all married and on their own, eleven grandkids, and two great-grandkids. This December it will be 46 years.

I Remember

One day my wife was telling our grandkids Bible stories while she was looking for pictures to teach her Sunday school class. The kids started to ask about the pictures and what they meant. She told about Joseph and his brothers, how his brothers mistreated him, and what had happened to him. God turned what was a bad situation into something good.

I remembered how at the age of five I had a similar thing happen to me. We were in a revival at Hubbard Missionary Baptist Church. Some people were being blessed by God and they were doing better. But at the age of five, I didn't know much about the Lord's blessings. All I knew was that I was seeing a lot of people there and what my grandmother had told me. I told her that I felt that I wanted to follow Christ and to be like one of his disciples. I feel now it was the Holy Spirit dealing with me. I guess my grandmother dismissed the thought of a five year old knowing anything about being saved.

She simply said, "You have to give up everything to follow Jesus."

This I have learned in my Christian life. What you give up is not worth having in comparison to what you gain from knowing Jesus. I'm blessed beyond measure. I heard a lady singing a song one time. The song said, "If Jesus never came back, I will praise Him for bringing me from where I was to where I am today."

That says it all to me. I'm so blessed to follow Him.

Mayor of Poduch

In the 1950's, in the big metropolis of Poduch, Texas which had a population of about 2,000 or a little better, a very comical thing happened.

Like most small towns they had their town drunks and gossip centers at the drugstore or the big barber shop where the men hung out. The beauty shop was for the women. It wasn't uncommon for phones to be on fire from use if someone found out something on someone else in town that was supposed to be hush-hush. They had the town floozies and the ladies' men who thought God had made women entirely for them personally and would chase a skirt regardless who it was on. Of course, every town has it's kind of 'off the rocker,' not thinking too straight or as some called it the town idiot.

Well, Poduch was no different. But they had 2 people that came under this category. They had Tommy Wilson. Tommy had about 6 or 7 kids who, in later years turned out to be very bright. One of his sons turned out be a college instructor for computer science and taught math. Tommy lived off welfare and as far as I know never held a job. They also had Lela Carmichael. Now both of these people didn't know what a bath tub was for, and they wore the same clothes day after day until they practically fell off. But there was a big difference in Tommy and Lela. Tommy never held a job, but Lela was a workaholic. She hauled garbage for the city businesses and was always tight with her money. She lived in a shack on the edge of town. It was said she owned about 1/3 of the commercial buildings in Poduch. I know for a fact she owned the building the post office was in at that time. But to look at her, she was a homeless person on the street.

They said when she died and they started tearing down her old house that they found money stuffed in the walls. She had been rat holing it for years.

The city was having an election for mayor and city councilmen. One of the good old boys thought how funny it would be to put Tommy's name in as running for mayor. He paid the filing fee for him. All of this was unknown to Tommy. But when he saw his name on the list of people running for mayor, he was beside himself with pride.

The day came for the election. The entire town was laughing about Tommy going to be mayor. What a sight that was! Everyone was voting for Tommy out of it being a big joke. Someone started asking around, and it seemed Tommy was getting more votes than anyone else. So the big joke was getting more serious all the time. The good old boys had to start knocking on doors and begging people to come and vote to keep Tommy from getting in office. If Tommy had gotten into office in Poduch, it would have been the laughing stock of the Four States Area. Of course, they could have had a recall election, but still it would have made the news and some of the good old boys would have looked awful foolish with egg on their face. Well, it turned out Tommy didn't get into office, but he only missed it by a hundred or so votes.

The good old boys thought about pulling some of their jokes again, but not in an election.

Jokes were a way of life for some in this small town of Poduch because it was their entertainment. I always hated for it to be at the expense of someone else.

My Granddad

My granddad was born on May 3, 1900. It was near a small community known as County Line about 20 miles south of De Kalb, Texas. This part of north east Texas was still wild in most ways. Men still carried pistols on their hips and used them sometimes. The earliest thing I remember him telling me was about the time he spent in west Texas at about the age of 19. A group of boys went out to west Texas from this area.

He met a girl out there and got into a fight over her. He lost the fight and left shortly after that. I was going through some of his pictures after my grandparents' deaths and found one that said on the back "My West Texas Gal."

Let me tell of a very strange thing that happened to me. While I was driving a truck in 1975, I had delivered a load of lumber to Odessa, Texas. On my way back I stopped at a truck stop at Big Spring. The café was full. So I asked some old ranchers if they would mind if I sat down with them. It was about the only seat left. They asked me where I had been, and I told them. Then they asked me where I was from.

I said "I'm from Texarkana," thinking they probably wouldn't know where the town of De Kalb was.

One of them popped up and said "Yeah, I know where Texarkana is. I was raised just west of there.

"Where?" I asked.

He said, "De Kalb."

I said, "That's my hometown."

He said, "I was raised in a small community named Hodgeson."

Then I said, "I was raised at Hubbard," which is another community only a few miles down the road.

159

Come to find out, he was one of the young teenage boys that came out to west Texas with Granddad in 1919. Now what chance would you give to two people meeting like that?

After my Granddad came back to north east Texas he met my grandmother, and they got married soon thereafter.

My granddad would do anything for a dollar. Back in those days you had to do just about anything. Times were hard. I remember him telling me about going to town every Saturday. That's when all the horse traders would gather and try to cheat one another. It was always held at the same place, just south of the railroad track at the wagon yard. They could circle the wagons to make a rodeo area. Some of them might have an old bronc of a horse that they wanted to see how well it was broken. My granddad would ride those old bronc horses and mules. They put a harness collier on the horse for him to hold on to. If he did well on riding the broncs, they would pass the hat. That was how he made some of his money. Most of the time the broncs weren't broke, but Granddad was.

From 1921 until 1936 it was hard times. In that time frame he had been a prison guard, a farmer, and a livestock trader. He also cut railroad crossties off of his land to pay for his mortgage and to make a partial living. He bought about a hundred acres 3 miles south of DeKalb in the Hubbard Community. By 1939, he had built a house. Things really begin to improve for him around that time. Red River Arsenal was being built by Brown & Root. He was hired as a carpenter, but he didn't last long at that. One day the General foreman came by, looked at his work, and asked what he was supposed to be. My granddad said, "A carpenter."

The foreman said, "Not any longer. Come along with me." From then on he was the time keeper. One thing for sure is my granddad was not a carpenter. Apparently, he did have contacts with good carpenters though because he had someone build my uncle a good solid oak desk which I still have.

After Red River Arsenal, my granddad got on as a guard since he had guard experience. I remember him telling me he had to fight to stay awake on graveyard shift which is normally from 11 pm to 7 am. He said he would chunk rocks to stay awake. He told me about an officer that he had found at the end of a building who was so drunk that he had fallen off the steps and had hurt his face something fierce. My granddad was supposed to have reported it, but he picked him up and did what he could for him as far as getting him cleaned up. He got someone to get him to a doctor without anyone knowing about the drunkenness. Apparently there was a lot of partying going on in some areas at Red River Arsenal and Lone Star Army Ammunition Plant during WWII.

Right after the war was over; my granddad quit work and started making his living as a livestock trader until he died in 1971. He always had money, so he must have done pretty well at it, plus he was never one to go and blow money either.

About that same time I came along. On March 4, 1946 at 8:30 am my granddad had gone to feed the hogs and other stock. He came back and asked if my mom was ok. My grandmother said, "Yeah, she's fine. She just had a boy." So I was born in my grandparents' house, and I still have the bed I was born on.

My grandparents' house was second home to me. My grandmother baby sat me. They had an old ditch out in the pasture where metal cans and glass were thrown to keep the dirt from washing away. I was 6 years and was out there where I shouldn't have been, but it was a great place to play.

It was also a place to get a cut foot. I was out playing around it one day when I cut my foot. My brother, Choice, helped me to the house. I was bleeding profusely. We made it to the front porch. My grandmother, who we called Ma, came to see about me. She told my brother to go get the alcohol. Well, he did get it, but when he came back and saw all the blood, he passed out. Ma had to leave me and go and see about him.

In my childhood if you had a cut, the first thing you got was a good dose of alcohol to keep down infection. This usually brought on a lot of screaming because it burned. I survived, but I still have a scar on my foot from the deep cut.

My Grandparents House

About 1939 my granddad either got a grant to buy more land or received a good loan from the bank. I was under the impression that he got a grant from the government because he didn't care much for banks. I also heard that President Roosevelt made it easy for farmers and ranchers to get loans from the Federal Government.

My grandmother said, "Banks will cheat you by charging you an outrageous amount of interest for a loan, but only give you a little interest if you have your money in their bank."

As soon as my grandparents had bought the land, they began thinking about building a house. It was about 3 miles south of De Kalb, Texas on then Texas Highway 26. It has since been renamed U.S. 259. It was near the Hubbard Chapel Community.

They asked my grandmother's brother, Will Shumake, to build the house. He was from the old school of carpentry. He laid out the foundation, put up a rough 2"X4" on each end of the foundation, and put a 2X4 on top, started nailing rough 1X12s running parallel to the 2X4s on the end, and nailed it to the foundation. The house had only one wall thickness at this time. They made a paste out of flour and water and then put it on the inside walls to hang the wallpaper. After several layers of newspaper to cover up the cracks in the wall, it had a coat of paint put on it.

After a certain period of time, they covered the rough pine outside walls with shiplap lumber and painted it white. It was built with two flues, one for the kitchen and one for the living room. However, they always used butane and propane for heating and cooking. My granddad had had enough of cutting firewood in the past.

In 1952, my grandparents had something a lot of other people didn't have at that time, and that was a telephone. If you lived on a highway you could get one. They lived on the highway, but we didn't.

It was a tradition that my grandmother would make a trip to Texarkana a least once a year for the purpose buying what they called linoleum for each room as it wore out. But it wasn't linoleum, as we know it today; it wasn't any more than thick oilpaper with a flowered pattern on it. They wore out quickly with all the dirt my granddad would bring in on his feet. Of course, I didn't help either with what I brought in.

There was a living room, dining room, kitchen, three bedrooms, front and back porch, and a path to the outhouse. One of the bedrooms was a summer room for easy and cool sleeping. It had two windows on each of the three sides facing out with oak trees shading it.

At one time they had a smoke house in the backyard where they kept hams and canned vegetables and fruits. My grandmother had a washhouse in the backyard also where she had her wringer washer with all of the tubs that were required for it. It was barely big enough for one person to get in much less two people. Washday was a major deal to her. Prior to having the washhouse, I saw my grandmother and Mom build a fire under an old black wash pot, get it blistering hot, put in lye soap, and scrub clothes on a washboard. It was hard work, but the clothes came out spotless white.

In 1955, they had a carpenter tear out two walls of the living room and kitchen doing away with the dining room. This made a more comfortable living area. About that same year, my granddad had a two-car garage built with a small room that ran the full length of the building in the back.

In 1963, they had a carpenter build an indoor bathroom, and they got plumbing for the first time. At this time, they had a new well dug. It wasn't any better water that the old well. They really had a problem with the water. It had so much calcium and lime in it that it was hard to drink and left a residue on every glass and anything else it came in contact with. I don't know why they built where they did because up the hill was an old house place with water that was much better than theirs.

The old house was built the old fashion way, but it must have been built well because as of this writing in 2005 it is still standing.

On Fire

Billy was really hurting from his hemorrhoids again. He got up around 3 o'clock in the morning to put some Preparation H on them to get some relief. It was dark, but he didn't turn on the lights. He didn't want to wake his wife, and he also felt if he turned the lights on, he wouldn't be able to go back to sleep himself. So, he reached for what he thought was Preparation-H. It wasn't. It was Ben Gay instead. Ben Gay is for tired and aching muscles with all the heat of liquid fire. As soon as he put it on his hemorrhoids, the lights did come on, and he was running and screaming in all directions. His wife liked to never have gotten him to slow down long enough for her to ask what the problem was.

"Honey, Honey what's wrong?" she said.

He was making laps around the house outside saying, "Oh! I'm burning up! Oh! I'm burning up! "

Finally after about half an hour, he was able to stop and sit down in a tub of cool water. But that was not total relief. He had to endure it until it wore off.

Billy said, "You know I haven't had any problems with hemorrhoids since then."

If only they had called me, I could have told them the solution to making it stop burning. You just rub ice on it!

I have learned something from this story: If you have a doubt of any kind, go ahead and turn the lights on to see what you have in your hand.

Our Dogs

I live in the country so I don't feel a need to keep my dogs put up. I feel a dog would a lot rather be free than pinned up. I'd rather not have one if I have to keep them pinned up. If they don't bother anyone I will let them run free. I know that's how I would feel if I were a dog.

One day in 1973 Terry, one of my best friends, asked me if I wanted Old Dot. He said he was going to have to get rid of her. He just didn't have room for her at his new place. So I said, "Sure I want her." Dot was a liver and white pointer birddog. She was good at what she did which was to point Bobwhite quail. Terry was thinking she was only 3 or 4 years old but come to find out she was much older than that—more like 7 or 8. I had a 1960 Volkswagen with the back seat out so I could put Dot in there when we went hunting. Terry did my mechanic work on the old Volkswagen.

Well, on this misty and cold February day, Terry and I were on our way to hunt, and I smelled something really bad. I looked over at Terry and asked him, "Did you do that?" He said, "No, but I was about to ask you the same question." Then we both looked back at Dot. Dot got the blame for that one. But she looked so innocent.

One day, we were hunting down near the Red River bottoms. Dot pointed a covey of Bobwhite quail in a switch cane thicket. Well, these birds wouldn't flush. So Dot went in after them with me right behind her. I saw her chasing after them trying to make them flush. They were running in circles, and she was trying to put her paws on them. She tried to reach down and bite them, but they were too fast. They finally did flush, but we didn't get a good shot. It was the funniest thing watching her pawing those birds. I'll bet she

167

put her paw down 10 times in 10 seconds. They weren't moving much just enough to keep her from getting them.

My wife Cynthia was mixing up some hot rolls from scratch, but she used old yeast so they didn't rise. She threw about 5 dozen out the back door. When I came home from work, I noticed Dot wasn't looking too well. I asked my wife what was wrong with Dot. She said, "I bet she ate all those rolls I threw out the back door." Dot would groan and just look pitiful.

If a dog could talk, I believe Dot would have said, "I feel terrible from gobbling up all those rolls." But she survived that one.

One thing I know, I sure loved and still miss Old Dot. I never found another birddog as good as she was. Besides being loving and willing to please, she was just a good dog.

After Dot we had several more dogs, but for years they were getting run over on the highway. We buried them on "Doghill" right behind the house.

We had just got rid of Old Suzy. For some reason she didn't like kids. She wasn't my favorite, so she hit the road to the pound. I had told my son Brian that we would get another one. We went to the city pound looking for a Chow puppy. I wanted one that would protect the family. They had some that were half Chow and half Lab pups. Brian said, "Let's pick that one." But I said, "No, let's look at all of them and get the one that looks more like a Chow." We got one out of the corner that was asleep. He was solid black. We took him straight to the vet and got him all his shots. They asked what his name was, so we named him Joe. Joe lived 10 years and was just what we wanted, a good protector. He wouldn't necessarily bite; he would just make you think he was going to bite you, which was good because I don't want anyone to be bitten. My son Brian taught him to obey. He would hook Joe up in a harness and let him pull small tree limbs. They had a good time together, and they were best buddies. Where Brian went, Joe wasn't far behind. Joe was the protector of my wife also. Many times he would get in between her and other dogs and people. A lot of times there were just too many of them to fight off.

One time my wife had to go and rescue Joe. A dozen or more dogs had Joe down in a ditch and wouldn't let him up. They just keep on chewing on him. She drove them off and brought him home. He was sure stove up for a while after that fight.

In February of 2001, he finally lay down and died after 10 years of long life. My wife and I both cried over loosing Joe. I sure wanted another Joe, but I haven't found one yet that measure up to him.

We went looking for another Chow. I found Old Bear at the city pound. He was full blood Chow with papers. He was supposed to be only 2 years old, but we suspect he was much older. When I first saw him, I thought he was too mean to be for us, but come to find out he was just scared. After I got him home, he settled down. He looked like he could chew you up in one bite and spit you out in the next. But he wouldn't bite anything but a biscuit. Old Bear didn't last too long. He was close to being blind and deaf, and he like to lie out on the highway. That's where my son found him. He didn't chase cars; he just liked to lie near the road. Why I don't know. It sure broke my heart, but I realized the price of freedom sometimes comes high. It did for Old Bear.

My daughter, Tami, picked up Abby, who is a German Shepherd and Chow mix, from a shelter in Longview. Abby is a home-body for sure. She never gets on the road. But she will bark at strange things. She is still around and will be for a while because she is cautious and stays where she belongs.

Brian knows I like Chows so for my birthday he picked up a ¾ Chow and ¼ wolf pup who we call Babe. I think she is going to be one of those biscuit eaters. We just have to wait and see because she is only 6 months old.

As you can tell by now, I love dogs and always feel like they are my best friend. Cats on the other hand are good to have around, but they can never be your best friend.

Possum Jackson

I never met the man, but I heard a lot about him. He was Possum Jackson. He graduated from James Bowie High School in about 1960. He was the brother-in-law to a cousin of my mine. But I really don't know if he claimed it or not. They said he had a head as hard as brick, maybe harder. When he learned he could butt things with his head, he was into showing out a lot. He would butt kids' car doors and bend them in.

I had a college instructor that had been Possum's coach in high school. One day when the coach walked into the dressing room of the gym, another player was holding a trashcan up daring Possum to butt it with his head.

The coach said, "Put that trashcan down."

The player said, "Coach I wasn't going to really let him hit it. I was going to pull it away at the last second and let him butt the wall."

The old James Bowie School was built back in the 1930s. The WPA built it out of stone from the surrounding area.

The coach said, "You were honestly going to let him hit his head against that wall."

The player said, "Yeah, everyone knows Possum's head is hard as a rock."

The coach said, "Don't let me catch you doing this again. His head may be hard, but it's not that hard."

The player said, "I don't know coach. It's pretty hard."

I think Possum was a pretty fair football player. With a head like that how could he not be one? The last time I heard anything about Possum, he hadn't used his head too well.

171

The FBI had him on counterfeiting charges, and he was going to spend some time in the big house. I guess he never learned crime doesn't pay. He should have used what's inside his head.

172

Rotten Apple in Every Barrel

My great-great-grandfather Nathan was a rotten apple if there ever was one.

Nathan's father, John, was a Regimental Sergeant in the Revolutionary War. He was an honorable man but couldn't read or write at all. He was born in 1752 in Virginia but moved to West Virginia. Later he moved to Winchester, Indiana, where his son Nathan was born.

After he was grown and in business for himself, Nathan had to leave Indiana in the middle of the night because his customers at his gristmill found out he was cheating them. So he left his financial affairs to his brother-in-law who was a much respected lawyer. Besides being a cheat, Nathan was also a counterfeiter.

Sometime about 1836 Nathan moved to Benton, Arkansas, and his father moved with him. They stayed there about 5 years. Then in 1841, the family moved to Red River County, Texas, while Texas was still a country and not a state. Later he came to

Bowie County after Red River County was divided. They were the third white family to be in the western end of Bowie County. He bought 2 sections of land at 50 cents per acre. That was 1,280 acres. However, the land was all in timber, and he had no way of making a living here. So he ran off another batch of money on his printing press and went to New Orleans, Louisiana. There he bought 6 slaves for $3,750 with counterfeit money. Any time he needed a big amount of money, he would make his own. He brought the slaves back up to Bowie County and probably worked them nearly to death clearing land of timber.

No sooner had he done this than he decided he didn't like it there. He picked up a book on how to be a doctor or a dentist. He moved to Little River County, Arkansas, and became a doctor. He changed his last name to Bell. But this time he didn't take his family with him. He left his many kids, a wife, and his father to fend for themselves. That's what I call a low down rotten apple if I have ever heard of one.

St. Michael Hospital Waiting Room

In 1986, my dad had bypass heart surgery. My brother and I both stayed in the ICU waiting room at St. Michael Hospital during the night to let our mom go home and get some much needed rest. But I stayed the first night because my brother had traveled from Tyler, Texas, after working all day.

I got out of the shower, changed into fresh clothes, and grabbed a pillow and a blanket. I was in a hurry and grabbed an old blanket with ragged edges because it was the first thing handy. I was running late getting to the hospital, so I jumped into my pickup truck and took off. When I got there to relieve my brother in the ICU, the waiting room was nearly full. There was only one Lazy Boy recliner left, so I got in it quickly. As I was carrying my pillow and blanket over to put them down, some good old boys who looked like they hadn't missed too many meals in their lifetime made a comment about my old ragged blanket. There were two brothers and a sister in this family.

One of the brothers said jokingly, "You must have taken it off your horse after you tied him up down in front of the hospital parking area."

They were really carrying me high about the old blanket for a spell. I went and had supper, quickly got back, and settled down for a good night's sleep in those comfortable recliners. After chatting a little bit with this family and finding out where they were from and what was wrong with their mom, I realized that they were really regular folks just like me.

About midnight I was awakened by the noise of snoring by these two good old boys. They had a duet going. It was loud enough to rattle the pictures off the walls. I lay there for an hour trying to get back to sleep but couldn't until I got sleepy enough. They finally settled down with their snoring. The next morning the nurses woke us up saying, "Ya'll can go in and see the patients. Visitors are permitted now."

I was stretching after a night of interrupted sleep. I was aiming to get even with the good old boys about all the ribbing they had given me about my old blanket. I got up from the recliner, went over to the closest brother's recliner, and looked all around it on both sides and in back of it, like I was looking of something.

He asked, "Have you lost something?"

I said, "No, I was just wondering if I could find any saw dust over here from that sawmill you had in operation last night."

He asked, "What do you mean?"

I said, "With all that snoring you must have really cut some logs, and there must be some saw dust left."

The good old boy's sister and the rest of the waiting room died out laughing about what I said. Of course, the ones I pulled it on didn't think it was so funny, but I was determined to get them back. It was all in fun, we enjoyed the antics of it all, and it passed the time away.

My dad did make a full recovery from the surgery and was still going strong at the age of 90.

The Home Coming Party

One day my grandmother told me a story about when she and my granddad were first married. It was 1923. My mother was about a year old at the time. My granddad had been to town one Saturday afternoon. He had a little too much to drink with the boys. I can just imagine him having to ride that old mule 10 or 12 miles home. That was about the only way they had of getting anywhere because they didn't have a car of any kind. A car probably wouldn't have made it down some of the roads that he had to travel. Riding that far sober was one thing, but doing it drunk was another. He came home drunk with a hangover and was telling my grandmother that she ought get the shotgun and just shoot him.

He said, "I'm a not good husband, not a good father, not a good provider."

Quite the opposite was true considering the economy, circumstances of life, and just the times in which they lived. He did the best he could at doing all these things. The way he felt right at that moment he regretted ever touching a bottle. But right then he felt like he was just an old sorry drunk. "Bessie, you ought to just shoot me." He kept saying this over and over. He was sitting on the front porch holding his head in his hands. It wasn't long before my grandmother came around the corner of the house with a shotgun.

She said, "Well, Jewell, if you say I ought to shoot you, being the good wife that I am, I'm sure going to do what you say."

He still had his head in his hands. He looked up, saw her with that gun, and said, "Bessie, put that gun down."

She said, "No! I am going to shoot you just like you

said."

He was off and running for his life in a split second and she was chasing him. They ran around the house for a while until one of them gave out. I don't think the shotgun had a shell in it, but he didn't know that. He could see she was as mad as an old wet hen. She made him think she would shoot him and that's what counted because he didn't come home drunk anymore. In all the twenty five years I knew my granddad, I never saw him drunk. I saw him take a drink, but never saw him drunk.

My granddad was a livestock trader. One day we were working to get one of his old cows up that was down sick and couldn't get up and walk. He was trying to hoist her up to get her to stand. We had worked and worked on this old sick cow.

All of sudden he said, "I've got to go to the house. I'm worn out. My nerves have had it." I had noticed he had the shakes a little.

The first thing he did was to get a shot glass, fill it up, take a drink, and refill it again. That was all it took. His nerves were settled down again. But as hard as we worked, we never did get that cow up.

He could have done like another cattleman that had the same problem that I had heard about. Every day for about a month the man had been giving his old cow molasses and whiskey to keep her strength up with the hope of getting her up on her feet so she would be of some value. One day he went to see about her. When the cow saw him, she started mooing for her fix of molasses and whiskey drink. She had gotten to be an old drunk herself. Why would she want to get up with the royal treatment of a nice warm barn to stay in, plenty of hay to eat, and not having to do anything but get her molasses and whiskey every day? The old cattleman remedied the problem shortly thereafter.

That gives me more inspiration to get up if I'm sick, not to lie down and get comfortable, and to never come home drunk. My wife has already promised to remedy that problem.

My granddad wasn't a church going man at all. I was concerned about him and his salvation, so I had my pastor go by and have a talk with him. He had been in the hospital, but he gotten better and was doing his normal thing of working with cows. My mom told me that he knew his time wasn't long for this world, and he would lie on his bed and talk to the Lord. I think he had an opportunity to do something some people don't have and that was time to make peace with Jesus. On January 6, 1971, he passed away at a livestock auction barn, one of his favorite places to be. I think he would have wanted it that way. It left a void in my life that I have never been able to fill. It will be nice to have fellowship with him again someday in heaven.

Twins

They say everyone has a twin in this world. Well, people I have worked with over the years say I have one.

I had just received a promotion at Red River Army Depot to Facilities Division, driving a dump truck and operating a variety of other equipment. Being the jokester that I am, I was always picking a humorous argument with the security guards, and likewise, they were ready and willing to argue back. Since I had just started driving a truck and saw Dave several times a day, he thought this truck coming through the gate was me and decided to go out and stop the truck as one of his antics.

He said to the driver in a sarcastic way, "Let me see your badge."

Dave reached up, snatched the badge away, and started to write it down on his roster. He noticed the badge didn't have my name on it.

He said to the driver, "Sorry about that. I thought you were someone else."

Dave asked the driver if he was thinking about saying something back to his smart remark. The driver said, "Not as long as you have that pistol on your hip."

Another incident of having a twin happened about a year later. I was taking my afternoon break in the canteen area drinking a soda. A group of ladies that worked in a nearby office walked in and sat down.

One of them asked me, "How come you're not on vacation like you're supposed to be?"

I said, "Because I'm not supposed to be on vacation. And I don't think you know me."

She said, "Yeah, I know you. Your wife is my cousin."

I said, "Lady, you don't know me."

I got up and left before I got in a fight over who I was and what my real name was. I've seen this fellow since this incident. Naturally, I think I'm the better looking of the twins.

You Might Be A Redneck If

In Jeff Foxworthy words, "You might be a redneck IF" you do some crazy country things. My wife thought this was an example where 'You Might Be a Redneck If' would apply.

One Sunday my wife, my dad and I were having lunch at Granny's cafe in Hooks, Texas, as it was our custom to do after church. Granny was about to close for the day when a fellow walked in. He wanted lunch before he went fishing.

He asked, "Ya'll still open?"

Granny said reluctantly, "Yeah, come on in."

Granny's sister-in-law who was the waitress was sitting down and complaining, "Oh my back is killing me."

This fellow that just walked in and sat down said, "I can help your back. I'm a Chiropractor. Come on down to my office tomorrow."

She said, "No, I need help right now. How about a free treatment?"

The doc said, "I really need a pillow for her head to rest on."

My wife said, "I have a pillow in the car."

The chiropractor said, "Could I borrow it for a couple of minutes?"

"Sure you can borrow it." Then my wife leaned over to me and whispered; "Now we have an excuse to stay--to get my pillow back. I wouldn't miss this show for anything in the world."

The doc said, "Ok, get your tail up on that table then."

They pulled two tables together which I knew was a disaster waiting to happen. We had to get up and give them our table since it was the only long table in the restaurant. It was ok because we were through with our lunch anyway.

He started pulling and twisting her. With the tables not being stable, he nearly dumped her on the floor. He pulled and twisted popping her back for a period of time. Finally he said, "Well, that's about all I can do for you. How is your back feeling now?"

She said, "Yeah, much better." She got up and went about her business.

I agreed with wife, "Only a redneck would enjoy a show where a chiropractor would give a free back treatment on a café table."

I was sorry to see Granny's go out of business. They had good food, and it was a good place for redneck entertainment.

Words of Encouragement

I'm convinced God wanted me to write a few words down for people to find Jesus.

The pastor I was saved under was a fine person named Othel. He was on fire for the Lord. This is one of the stories that he told me.

He had a brother named Leonard. Leonard was always in trouble of one kind or another and was not saved. Othel was desperate about getting his brother saved because he was getting into deeper trouble all the time.

One day he went to see his mother who was a Christian and made this statement to her: "Mom, let's get down on our knees and ask God to do whatever it takes to save Leonard."

Well, it wasn't long before Leonard was arrested for armed robbery. He was sentenced to 20 years in Huntsville. As many of you know, the Texas State prison at Huntsville is no playhouse. It's one of the toughest prisons in the nation. Leonard was saved while in prison. Just because Leonard was now a Christian didn't mean he was getting any special privileges. He still served about 5½ years of his twenty-year sentence.

So if you have someone that is hard to reach for Christ, you may pray this same prayer. God may take someone that you love or put them in a world of pain to get them to where Jesus can deal with them. Don't pray the prayer if you are halfhearted about it. God takes prayer serious. So should we.